SEATTLE VICE

STRIPPERS, PROSTITUTION, DIRTY MONEY, AND NARCOTICS IN THE EMERALD CITY

RICK ANDERSON

SASQUATCH BOOKS
SEATTLE

FOR MO

Printed in the United States of America
Published by Sasquatch Books
Distributed by PGW/Perseus
15 14 13 12 11 10   9 8 7 6 5 4 3 2 1

Cover photographs: Frank Colacurcio: AP/Wide World Photos/Gary Stewart,
                   Aurora Avenue: Spike Mafford/Stockbyte/Getty Images,
                   Go Go Dancer: ©Frugo/Dreamstime
Cover design: Rosebud Eustace
Interior design and composition: Sarah Plein

Library of Congress Cataloging-in-Publication Data

Anderson, Rick, 1941-
   Seattle vice : strippers, prostitution, dirty money, and narcotics in the Emerald City / Rick Anderson.
      p. cm.
   Includes bibliographical references and index.
   ISBN-13: 978-1-57061-661-7
   ISBN-10: 1-57061-661-2
   1. Crime--Washington (State)--Seattle--History. 2. Criminals--Washington (State)--Seattle--History. 3. Vices--History. 4. Political corruption--Washington (State)--Seattle--History. I. Title.
   HV6795.S5A53 2010
   364.109797'772--dc22
                              2010032548

Sasquatch Books
119 South Main Street, Suite 400
Seattle, WA 98104
(206) 467-4300
www.sasquatchbooks.com
custserv@sasquatchbooks.com

CONTENTS

Author's Note

In the eighties, convicted racketeer Frank Colacurcio Sr. told me that mob stories about him were made up. "Fairy tales," he said. Twenty years later, with a few more prison stretches to his name, he told me, "Organized crime, you just never had it here." If he meant the Mafia, true; if he meant himself, he was likely saying his crimes were sometimes disorganized, as his conviction rate indicates: seven felonies, one reversed.

His mob did incorporate some of the structural elements of the Mafia, or at least the Army—loyal volunteers willing to do mayhem, have sex, and drink beer. As future U.S. attorney general Robert F. Kennedy indicated in the fifties and Seattle mayor Greg Nickels said half a century later, Colacurcio was *some* kind of godfather. "I believe that there is organized crime involved in at least that club and perhaps others," the mayor said of Frank's flagship nudie joint in Seattle. Frank laughed. "Oh, I think he's just trying to win an election," he told me. "It's not the old days anymore, I should know."

He did. In the vaginal valley of Seattle vice, Frank was the polluted river that runs through it. Drawing from the historic tributaries—bad cops, corrupt pols, cathouse madams, bookmakers, pornographers, and drug dealers, whose tales flow into his—the stripper king carried us from one Seattle century to the next, meandering through Tacoma, Portland, and the West. In the process, fact has blended with fiction, creating a Mafia mythology. But the preponderance of evidence—Frank's central, decades-long role in the vice rackets and as head of an operation that reached into ten Western states and many of their prisons— affirmed his place as a unique American crime figure. His story is told in hundreds of thousands of pages of law enforcement and court documents and the background interviews I've had with investigators, attorneys, prosecutors, and Frank's friends and foes, in addition to historical research through books and newspapers and my own past encounters with him.

He notched his first felony, a sex-related charge, during the Roosevelt presidency. He was charged with his eighth felony, a sex-related charge, under the Obama administration. It is an endurance record in lawbreaking rivaling, if not besting, New York's legendary Mafia godfathers. Really, how many of them could boast they were under indictment at age ninety-three and still trying to get laid?

Prologue

When the task force of government cars and wagons rolled into Frank Francis Colacurcio's driveway and courtyard on a Monday morning in 2008, doors flew open and squads of local cops and federal agents poured out. They rushed to the entryway of the $1.2 million, sand-colored home with a swimming pool overlooking Lake Washington. The three-bedroom, quarter-acre ranch house, built in Frank's heyday fifties and remodeled in 2004, was tucked into the side of the hill above Sheridan Beach. Its southern exposure looked away from the prying traffic that typically flew past on Bothell Way Northeast in Lake Forest Park. That day, cars slowed outside the compound's wall as drivers gawked at the scene: with all the FBI jackets, it might have looked like a national security incident. In fact, the lead task force investigator formerly worked on the FBI's international terrorism squad. But while Frank may have been considered an enemy combatant of sorts, his record was more that of an underwear bomber.

The front door opened, and the legendary stripper king appeared. The godfather of what might be called Nudity Inc.— his half-century-old, once far-flung empire of topless and fully nude dance joints featuring lap dances and hand jobs—had been a squat, barrel-chested brawler with wavy black hair and a thing for gold medallions. Now, in the doorway, he was a bent and balding grandfather of ninety-one with chicken-fuzz hair, greeting his landing party in a bathrobe. "Search warrant," one of the feds said. No vice-raid virgin, Frank knew the drill. He stood back so the force could swarm in. Then he went to phone the lawyers.

His bathrobe didn't necessarily mean the old man had been roused from sleep. Rolled up in his robe pocket was $10,000, mostly in hundreds. He liked to be prepared. At his age, senior citizens tended to plan their day around activities that cause the least drooling and heart attacks. Frank liked to hit the bedroom floor running, cane in hand, anticipating drop-ins by one of his dancers. "He gets laid every night," recalled one of the young women from the strip joints he has been operating for more than forty years—in more recent times featuring full frontal, and "backal," nudity. Dancers said he had a standing (well, laying) offer: earn up to $1,000 a day working at home—his. "It's surprising that a guy so old still wants it so much," another dancer had told some of the investigators now pawing through Frank's papers and searching his cupboards. "He tried to get me to go and have sex with him for $500!"

It had to be tempting for his underpaid girls. In the eighties, tired of restrictive state liquor laws and nosy inspectors, Frank converted his dance joints to soda pop clubs. To make up for the lost revenue, he began charging his dancers to strip. They were required to pay "rent" of more than $100 a shift, which they had to earn back, hopefully with a profit, from table dances and tips. Some weren't successful and resorted to the hands-on approach. As one club manager told a dancer reluctant to have sex with a paying customer, "Well honey, you've got to get in there and compete."

Frank liked to fish and play cards, but a toss in the hay was life itself. If he couldn't participate, he could watch, sometimes cutting peepholes into walls at his clubs, ogling girls in the dressing rooms or spying on them having sex with customers in the bar. On one occasion, a dancer warned Frank that sex was getting rampantly in and out of hand in the secluded VIP booths at Rick's, his nightclub in Seattle, just up the road from his Sheridan Beach spread. "I think a couple girls are bad," she said. "They do the real dirty stuff." Frank stopped her right there. "Where are they?" he asked. "I need one!"

This was not unexpected from a man whose 38-foot fishing boat was named *4PLAY*. In the seven decades that law enforcement had been coming to his door, one way or another it was about sex. In 1943 it was a teen girl he was convicted of raping under the pretense of showing her the ghosts that haunted his family's Eastside farm. Sixty years later, it was a young woman whose nipple he decided to grab—because he could. He was in his late eighties then and still feeding off the breast. He arose each day wondering how to get girls, or get money to get girls, or how to get girls to sell sex to get him money to get more girls. His wife, twenty-three years his junior, put up with it for three decades, then sent him divorce papers in prison. He had taken to keeping a number of girlfriends and several sets of books—the ledgers he stuffed in his pockets and the ones he showed the IRS. He devised an accounting system he called "ins and outs," as he once explained to a jury, wherein a chunk of the untaxed profits flows in and out and ends up as "miscellaneous." That was partly why the feds showed up at his home that morning in 2008. They thought Frank was doing the ins and outs again, known as skimming, which had already earned him two of his five prison terms.

Frank was saying nothing. Maybe he was offended. Having money didn't always mean he embezzled it. His criminal record had forced him into so-called retirement—he preferred to be called a "consultant" to his own strip business—but he'd paid taxes on a lot of those millions too. Stocks, banks, and real estate could have a bad season, but a nude dancing concession is almost recession-proof, with a built-in stimulus. To Frank, the tax harassment—"this police business"—was petty. Once, in 2007, after he'd supposedly retired, one of his club managers was arrested with several dancers for vice infractions at Rick's. The manager called Frank from King County Jail to make sure he knew they needed bail. The dancers were busted for the usual touching and groping violations, the manager said.

"But," she added on the recorded jail phone, "we have one with a really funny charge, and we're not quite sure why."

"What was it?" Frank asked.

"They're saying it's prostitution," said the manager. "But it's not a girl that I usually have a prostitution charge on . . . Maybe she was arrested by mistake."

"Ohhh," said a seething Frank, "them bastards!"

As an iconic entrepreneur, Frank Colacurcio had nothing to do with making Seattle what it is best known for today: caffeine, software, airplanes, and books by mail. Of course, before his clubs switched to soda pop, he did supply Howard Schultz's coffee market with customers who needed sobering up. He contributed to Bill Gates's tech world by creating a small demand for government software to track his crimes and tomelike court records. He did fly on the jets of William Boeing's airline customers to many clubs and prisons in the West, and to San Francisco that one day to hang a guy out a hotel window. An eighth-grade dropout, he wasn't much of a market booster for Jeff Bezos. Still, unlike Amazon.com, Frank's start-ups always made money.

He rose from farm worker to CEO of one of the nation's oldest and most successful vice businesses, and by the time he hit ninety, in 2007, more than $1 million a month in revenues was flowing through club Bank of America accounts. So his was a criminal enterprise, as the feds called it. But who hasn't said that about big corporations everywhere? And were Howard, Bill, William, and Jeff willing to go to prison for what they believed in? Frank was, again and again.

Back when Gates and Paul Allen were sprouting peach fuzz and entering geekdom, Frank's fleshy nightclub enterprise already stretched from Seattle to the Southwest, Canada, Alaska, and Hawaii. The key ingredient, tits and ass, was supplied by the dancers from Talents West, the Seattle personnel agency run by Frank and his macho girlie men. He'd gotten in and out of the pinball and jukebox businesses, and began buying up restaurants and selling sex and booze to the mass market. He got a rolling start from a corrupt vice tolerance policy blessed by Seattle's City Hall and carried out by police headquarters in a unique kind of public safety campaign: in the belief that sin couldn't be stopped but could be controlled, Seattle cops "regulated" gambling, prostitution, and other vices in a civic shakedown that peaked in the fifties and sixties.

Though such vices and devices were illegal, they were nonetheless licensed and overseen by government. The level of police enforcement was undertaken on a sliding scale, based on how much some businesses were willing to pay cops and city officials in bribes and kickbacks in order to obtain licenses, avoid fines, and remain open. It was a freaky-deaky policy, legalizing illegality, and paid off handsomely for the corrupt. Politicians larded their war chests, and cops stored stacks of cash in their attics. The Seattle police vice squad alone was collecting $6,000 in monthly payoffs from operators, taking a cut and distributing the rest up the rotted food chain. An otherwise conservative and industrious blue-collar town with the imagination to build a floating bridge and a Space Needle was, at its heart, a decadent city on the take.

Frank grew up to see cops and politicians with their hands out and figured it to be a career move. He would wind up as the tolerance policy's poster boy—enforcer, extortionist, and reputed Italian American mobster to boot—then go to prison for it. Decades later he'd be caught up in another City Hall payoff scandal. But by then he'd mastered the art of corruption: after the scheme was exposed in 2003, Frank and his associates got their money back.

Not that he needed it. Frank made a fortune operating in the Mafia-free zones of the West. The outside family mobs considered much of it Frank's turf or perhaps not worth the effort. He dominated other regional vice lords as well, such as the dangerously screwball Carbone gang of Tacoma, the Elkins mob of Portland, and small-time operators around the Northwest. He worked with the Teamsters and their crooked Northwest leaders, including Dave Beck, and madams such as Ann Thompson, a wise businesswoman who convinced an expansion-minded Frank that, alas, even with support from all those horny Teamsters, whorehouses wouldn't be profitable in undersexed Portland. He helped create a regional environment of sin and corruption for others, including Nellie Curtis, Seattle and Aberdeen's most memorable cathouse madam, and a former Miss Washington, Rose Marie Williams, whose hobbies were sewing, swimming, and screwing most of King County. Of course, Frank outpimped them all, with legions of his club girls servicing thousands of his eager customers over the years in VIP rooms and parking lots. The yellow brick road to today's Emerald City is littered with his strip club condoms.

Unlike his fellow Seattle CEOs today, Frank never earned a spot on the *Forbes* 500s, his fortune regularly plundered by defense attorneys. But he'd always been a shy member of the filthy rich, and rode around in a used Lincoln Town Car piloted by a retired lounge singer. Like Gates, Chairman Frank eventually stepped down from his leadership role to concentrate on his own charity of sorts, Frank's Foundation for Wayward Girls. But his influence and persistence continued to dazzle observers— among them, tireless FBI agent Corey Cote, who tailed Frank for years and called him "patriarch of the criminal organization." Though Cote and other investigators discovered Frank rubbed elbows with a few Mafia figures during his career, they saw him as an independent contractor. They believed him when he said the Cosa Nostra talk was "Mafia malarkey," even if he seemed to dabble in it. A friend of his said Frank joked about being Seattle's Brando-like boss, and one former associate tells the story that a Colacurcio mobster once left a bloody horse's head in a foe's bed, mocking a scene from *The Godfather*.

Conversely, Frank tended to understate the facts. He wasn't violent and never hurt anyone, he insisted. Yet he had a felony assault conviction and once beat a man until he pleaded for his life. The vice rackets, for all their good times, were also bloody and now and then fatal. Frank was accused of associating with killers and orchestrating some whackings—cold-case detectives loosely linked him to four or five deaths. Sometimes targeted by other local gangsters, Frank kept a cache of guns around, and in bar fights he could swing a mean club.

The fact that he remained a free man didn't sit well with the sore losers of law and order. As this century began, they formed a local, state, and federal Task Force to Get Frank. It cost millions—something much of the public saw as a wasteful intrusion into the world of consenting adults—resulting in a whole new series of federal racketeering, money laundering, and prostitution charges against him. The massive collection of evidence included more than 120,000 pages of documents and assorted audio, video, and business records stored on almost 2,300 CDs and DVDs. One undercover officer made more than 160 visits to Frank's clubs in recent years, contributing an estimated $18,000 in taxpayer funds to Frank's bank account. He made no arrests, according to court papers, but he took notes.

Frank was pretty sore about the indictment. The cops came barging in with a warrant while he held his bathrobe closed, for gods sakes! Used to be they'd pay him off for a crime like this.

Go look at Seattle vice history; you'll see.

ORIGINAL SIN

Mad Dog, Chief of Police

"The prisoner is placed in a cell far removed from others, so his screams cannot be heard."

The recorded legacy of Seattle vice and corruption reaches back two centuries, to impresario and saloon pioneer John Considine, who helped introduce Seattle to drinks, debauchery, and risqué bare-belly dancer Little Egypt. He also memorably battled rival Alexander Pantages for Seattle's vaudeville turf, with both men stealing each other's acts and rising to eventual fame in Hollywood, Considine as a silent-film producer and head of an acting family, and Pantages as a movie mogul and theater chain owner. But it was Considine's hidden payments to beat officers that made lesser-known history, ranking among some of Seattle's first street-level bribes. Just as a corrupting racketeer named Frank Colacurcio would do half a century later while dominating his era's vices, Considine offered cops cash to look the other way as he violated Seattle's sin laws. Among statutes he paid to break was the 1894 "barmaid ordinance." The law prevented women from working where alcohol was served, and Considine clearly needed them at his People's Theater, in what is now Pioneer Square. The "box-house" saloon and card room featured female performers who danced, sang, and serviced a willing crowd, mostly lusty prospectors spilling into town during the Klondike Gold Rush.

Considine also ran three illegal betting parlors by paying fines and bribing cops under a vice tolerance policy that would appear, disappear, and reappear in Seattle throughout the next century. His cozy relationship with Seattle police chief C. S. Reed allowed him to monopolize the vice action for a few years until competitors, some formidable, bought in. Among them was gunslinger Wyatt Earp, described in 1899—eighteen years after the gunfight at O.K. Corral—by the *Seattle Star* as "a man of great reputation among the toughs and criminals, inasmuch as he formerly walked the streets of a rough frontier mining town with big pistols stuck in his belt, spurs on his boots and a devil-may-care expression upon his official face." His Union Club on Union Street thrived for more than a year until a city-wide crackdown drove him off to San Francisco. Only months after Earp departed, Considine's joints reopened.

He didn't get along as well with the next police chief, however, so he killed him. In a 1901 showdown, Considine shot the dislikable William Meredith three times after Meredith fired at him first, the chief's bullet described in one news report as "scraping along the back of Considine's neck and lodging in the arm of a messenger boy having sarsaparilla at a soda fountain." Considine's actions were deemed self-defense by a jury that took just three hours to decide they didn't like Meredith either.

Of course, if it was OK to kill the police chief, what did that mean for everyone else? Brevity. Life could end abruptly in the middle of a horse ride or poker game. And thanks in great deal to corruption, incompetence, and the free flow of booze and drugs, citizens could vanish almost as if they never existed. Records to that effect can still be found in yellowed bound volumes in the King County Medical Examiner's Office at Harborview Medical Center. They tell terse stories of early vice-related lives and deaths. The file on the first person to officially die in King County reads in its entirety:

Name, M.M. Murphy.
Age, unknown.
Residence, Railroad Saloon, foot of Main Street, Seattle.
Cause of death, an overdose of morphine with suicide intent.
Date: March 20, 1889.

The second person to die was also linked to suicide. The third, a steamboat man, went out "in the discharge of his duties" and drowned; the fourth was shot on the outskirts of Slaughter, now known as Auburn; and the fifth succumbed to "frequent and repeated doses of bad whiskey." In the strange shorthand of the day, a woman named Laura Oldham, alias Laura Sidney, "died from the effects of a debauch started about one week before," while Miss Edith Valentine committed suicide when she "shot herself over the Budweiser."

The most consistent notation on every page is that the coroner had collected his $10 fee; on some pages, the collected fee is the only entry.

Back then and throughout most of the next century, "police protection" was a double entendre and depended on how much dirty money a business operator could afford to pay. Among those who could was Madam Lou Graham, who started up a bordello in the 1890s. Thanks to two of the era's most dependable commodities—vice and corruption—Graham, by the turn of the century, had become one of the city's wealthiest residents and a major landowner. Her bawdy house at Third Avenue South and South Washington Street, where some of Seattle's most elite businessmen dropped their shorts, is still remembered by a plaque on a new building at the brothel site today. When she died at age forty-two of syphilis, Madam Lou was rumored to have left her fortune to the Seattle School District, though it actually went to relatives back home in Germany.

The police payoff system continued under Charles "Wappy" Wappenstein, Seattle's head cop from 1906 to 1907. He became security chief at Seattle's first world's fair, the Alaska-Yukon-Pacific Exposition in 1909, held where the University of Washington now stands. He was then reappointed chief in 1910 by new mayor Hiram Gill, an early believer in tolerance policies, if not outright corruption. Wappy immediately informed the madams of Seattle's thriving brothels they each owed $10 per harlot per month, payable to him or his beat officers.

As historian Murray Morgan recalled in *Skid Road*, there were at least five hundred women working the old-town brothels, and Wappenstein made certain every one of them paid promptly: "The cops who patrolled the Skid Road were required to make periodic reports on the number of girls in each house. An occasional patrolman made trouble by raiding an establishment where protection had been paid, or by engaging in a shakedown on his private initiative, but such mavericks were quickly transferred to outlying residential districts or put to pound beats along the windswept stretches of the waterfront. Wappy had everything under control."

Mayor Gill didn't. He left town one day, and an acting mayor quickly formed a committee to investigate Seattle's vice. The *Seattle Post-Intelligencer* (*P-I*) also investigated and spread the word about City Hall corruption—just as it would do again fifty years later, exposing yet another corrupt regime of cops and politicians who "tolerated" vice in return for bribes and kickbacks. Gill was tossed out of office by voters in 1911. The deciding ballots came from women whose right to vote—briefly granted, then taken away in 1887—had only recently been restored. Wappenstein also lost his job and was indicted by a grand jury. That, too, would be the fate of the city's police chief half a century later, except that, unlike Wappy, he wouldn't go to prison.

Seattle vice flowed on unabated but less conspicuously. The city's first and only female mayor, Bertha Landes, failed to fully clean up corruption in the twenties—the housewife mayor called her effort "municipal housekeeping." She was up against a new round of payoffs and protection rackets that flourished around rum-running and bottle clubs during Prohibition. Corruption spread beneath her feet, as did abuse. When not on the take, cops were on the give, dishing out punishment not only to the guilty but also to the merely accused. Getting someone to confess to a crime meant simply putting them in a rowboat with an iron ball chained to their neck and riding them out onto the water. They could either talk or accidentally be thrown overboard. That was the procedure according to William Severyns, Seattle police chief from 1922 to 1926. In his autobiography, *Confessions of a Chief of Police*, Severyns, known as "Mad Dog," laid out what was an early version of waterboarding, giving murder suspects the "Ride Around the Lake."

> Two detectives enter the jail, perhaps posing as outraged relatives of the murdered person . . . The prisoner is seized roughly. A chain is fastened about his neck. From it descends a heavy iron ball.
>
> He is rushed out of the station and into a waiting automobile, which proceeds at high speed to the shores of Lake Washington. [The prisoner] is thrown into a rowboat and the putative avengers start to row toward the center of the deep and vast body of water.

Almost invariably the prisoner breaks down and either confesses to his participation, or tells what he knows of the identity of the real perpetrators.

In those days, cops multitasked with the iron ball, Severyns noted. They could balance it over a prisoner's head, attached to a cord threaded through a cell door and tied to the prisoner's raised leg. If he didn't confess and grew weary from questioning, his leg would give way and the ball would skull him. Police also used the "Electric Carpet." It was a live-wire mat that sent shocks, triggered by an interrogator, to any suspect thought to be lying. "In using this," Severyns cautioned, "the prisoner is placed in a cell far removed from others, so his screams cannot be heard." Should that fail, there was always brute force.

It is a method hard, direct and blunt—simply and crudely knocking a prisoner cold when he is caught in a deliberate lie. When the prisoner recovers consciousness, he finds the detectives standing over him, fists drawn back for more blows, and all shouting "Lie to us, you ———, will you?"

He didn't necessarily use or approve of these tactics, Severyns claimed, since they could be counterproductive. "So fearful was one man that he is said to have given the sheriff a confession not altogether true!" Severyns said he thought that was so unjust that the next year he ran for sheriff. And won.

In the late thirties, a stern mayor, and later governor, Arthur Langlie, pressed for new laws to combat corruption and abuse. A Republican, Langlie had such an impressive record he later wound up on a five-person list for the 1952 vice presidential nomination. Instead, Dwight Eisenhower chose the ethical time bomb, Richard Nixon. Yet Seattle vice and crime investigations still suffered from the shenanigans and incompetence of their practitioners. One, a man named Otto Mittelstadt, was the county's coroner in the thirties and forties and the inventor of the portable inquest. In reaction to an increasing number of automobile deaths, he began to convene coroner's proceedings outdoors at crash sites. He'd quickly call a judge, phone the media, and hurry all of them to the scene, where he'd assemble a jury on the street corner. There he'd swear in witnesses, then grill the hapless driver of the other car. While the practice was less bloody than some of those described by Severyns, the goal was much the same. "As the result of this policy," Mittelstadt said, "it often has been possible to obtain confessions from hit-run drivers and others who might have had time to frame a false defense, had the inquests been delayed."

Under different circumstances, that would be the fate of a budding young felon named Frank Colacurcio. He actually had time to think about it, but confessed anyway.

Ghost Farm

"Lawyer's First Client is Negro He Whipped in Prize Fight"

Young William Colacurcio arrived in America with his family from southern Italy and followed other relatives to the Northwest. It was the turn of the twentieth century, and the family raised crops near Bow Lake, on land just east of what is now Seattle-Tacoma International Airport, hauling fresh produce into Seattle and selling it at Pike Place Public Market. The Colacurcio clan also owned a farm on the Eastside, accessible by ferry or a long car ride around Lake Washington from Seattle in those pre–floating bridge days. William and his new wife, Christina, lived on the property, not far from what is now the Microsoft campus, but which back then sat in a hilly neighborhood of forests, fields, and narrow-lane roadways.

The birth of William and Christina's son, Frank Francis Colacurcio, on June 18, 1917, was the beginning of a love of labor. Over three decades, the sturdy Christina would give birth to five other boys (William Jr., Samuel, Victor, Daniel, and Patrick) and three girls (Rosie, Jessie, and Frances). At least six of the kids would one day wind up in the restaurant-and-bar business, and five of the boys would land in prison.

Frank was born during World War I and grew up in the flush postwar economy of the twenties. Along with his siblings, he learned a strict work ethic from his father, who toiled dawn to dusk tending crops and hauling them to market. With the Wall Street crash of 1929 and the ensuing Great Depression, Frank, like the other kids, was needed full-time in the field. At age fourteen, he quit school and went to work planting and harvesting produce and butchering livestock. In the thirties, he also worked a spell at the newly built Everett pulp mill. Eventually he and brothers Sam and Bill followed their father into the trucking and produce business, setting up a warehouse operation on Western Avenue at Madison Street, a few blocks south of the Pike Place Market.

A tough wise guy with a sense of humor, according to one relative, young Frank was working at the produce house one afternoon when a young girl came in looking for her sister, who also worked there. It was August 1942, and Frank, then twenty-five, got to chatting with the sixteen-year-old. They liked each other. When the girl learned her sister wasn't around, Frank offered her a ride. As the girl later recalled, Frank put it this way: "Do you want to see where the ghosts walk?"

Frank and his brothers had been spreading a story that their Eastside farm had recently been visited by a ghost. It was a made-up tale, but people seemed to believe it. The brothers told friends and visitors how they had tried to stalk a "milky shadow" that wailed and howled as it floated about their property, swooping through the barn and disappearing. They and others had tried to capture it, they said, but to no avail. The tale began to draw a crowd as word spread around the Eastside community. On one night alone, as many as three dozen self-appointed spook hunters turned up to help Frank and his brothers run around the grounds looking for the elusive apparition.

The girl was game and followed Frank to his truck. He steered toward Rainier Avenue and then through a new four-lane tunnel, paying a toll to cross the two-year-old Lake Washington Floating Bridge. Within the hour, they arrived at the ghost farm. Frank maneuvered up the driveway and headed directly into a garage. He got out, closed the garage door, and the two of them began kissing, then undressing. They had intercourse, the teen later told police.

Court records are unclear on how willing the teen had been. But she was a minor and Frank an adult, constituting a morals offense. The day after she spoke with police, the county prosecutor filed papers charging Frank with carnal knowledge, today known as statutory rape, and the story was in the next day's newspapers. That was the first mention of what has become sixty-eight years, and counting, of Frank's name appearing in print, and now online, wherein he was suspected, accused, tried, or convicted of a crime.

A story in the *P-I*, headlined "'Ghost'-Farm Brother Faces Morals Charge," reported that prosecutor B. Gray Warner had drawn up a complaint that led to the jailing of Frank on a $3,000 bond, a prohibitive amount to keep him in jail. The case might not have otherwise made the newspaper, but as the reporter wrote in the lead, Frank was "accused of attacking a 16-year-old girl Wednesday at the 'haunted' farm near Bellevue."

Frank hired an attorney and insisted the girl hadn't protested. The sex was consensual, he claimed. Later on, the girl brought up the nutty idea of marriage, and when he told her no way, Frank said, the girl indicated she'd tell police. Frank didn't think she was serious.

He apparently was prepared to do the right thing—which, to Frank, was go to prison rather than down the aisle. He was convicted the following year and sent to the Washington State Reformatory in Monroe, built in 1910 to house young offenders. In October 1943, the state parole board in Olympia set his term at two years. It didn't seem like much of sentence for rape, but parole officials (who set sentences back then) apparently didn't think it was much of a crime. They saved a more serious term, five years, for a man who had stolen a car.

Frank's first conviction wouldn't follow him around as much as would an association he struck up during that criminal case. His attorney was Albert Dean Rosellini, thirty-two, a law school grad from the University of Washington, who took the case, he said, as a favor to another Italian family. Rosellini, like Frank, was the son of immigrants. His father, Giovanni, had settled in Tacoma and with his kin ran a liquor business. Albert and his three sisters later moved with their parents to Seattle's Rainier Valley—known as "Garlic Gulch" for its concentration of Italian families. Two of Albert's cousins would become famous Seattleites—Victor Rosellini as a restaurateur and Leo Rosellini as a surgeon—but Albert became best known of them all.

When he represented Frank in court, Rosellini was in his tenth year of law practice. A onetime amateur boxer, he had gotten an immediate publicity boost just after hanging out his shingle, when he was hired to defend one of his former ring foes. The *Seattle Times* found the case a novelty. As the paper headlined it: "Lawyer's First Client is Negro He Whipped in Prize Fight." Rosellini later worked for King County prosecutor Warren G. Magnuson, who had graduated from UW Law four years before Rosellini and would go on to become one of the longest-standing members of Congress—a representative and senator from 1937 to 1981. Rosellini, too, entered politics and would endure inside and outside office for the next seventy years. In 1938 he was elected to the state Senate from the Thirty-third District: South Seattle and its suburbs. And in 1956, he was elected governor of the state of Washington.

Rosellini lasted two terms, until 1964, and might have made it three, in a seventies comeback attempt. But a last-minute press report did him in.

It said he was a friend of Frank's.

High Jinks and Whorehouses

"If I remember correctly, the headline actually said
'Man Bites Self to Death.'"

During and after World War II, vice still ruled, at least in some areas of downtown Seattle, which were off-limits to service members due to the prostitution and gambling. Not that sin was a bad thing. Seattle was a free spirit, a prospering timber and fishing town buzzed by Boeing airplanes, growing its economic reach. It was churchgoing and minor league, but still valued a frontier sense that rules were meant to be bent if not broken. That civic morality was notably recorded in the pages and newsrooms of the three daily papers: the Seattle *Times*, *Post-Intelligencer*, and *Star*, which folded in 1947. Though the facts tended to be whatever the cops said they were, the point of much of that era's journalism was to coax an appreciative laugh or maudlin tear from the reader, abetted by a sensational headline. With fresh ink rubbing off in their hands, subscribers could start the day reading pages of free obituaries about those who hadn't made it through the night. They could turn to an uplifting story about a woman who grew a potato that looked like Harold Stassen (a perennial candidate for president), thumb through the police blotter and columns of bowling scores, or go over the betting picks of young sports columnist Emmett Watson ("Army over Navy, Eggs over Easy, Curry over Rice"). They could view doctored photographs in which newsroom artists, using watercolor airbrushes, slimmed down the fat ankles of society matrons or removed the balls from German shepherds. They were family papers, after all.

In other words, newspapers were fun to read. And even more fun to work for. *Seattle Times* columnist John Reddin, recalling midcentury Seattle, wrote, "We rode the morgue wagon and sometimes took showers in the tiled shower room just off the big dormitory where deputy examiners slept when on all night duty." Both coroner Otto Mittelstadt and his successor, Johnny Brill, "ran a loose ship, as I recall, and we had some hilarious times in rather grim surroundings—the county morgue."

Vice and other crimes were the reporter's staples, and, unlike today, access to cops and records was rarely an issue. Newsmen, as even female reporters were known (when they weren't being called "sob sisters"), had entrée to the back corridors of police stations, hospitals, City Hall, and courtrooms, although occasionally a writer could get too close. Press seating was reserved for reporters in one court, in the basement of the old police headquarters on Yesler Way, the ornate flatiron building. The reporters' perch was next to where suspects stood, and members of the fourth estate sometimes found themselves mistakenly accused of theft, assault, and worse.

"On one occasion," Reddin recalled, "when the city attorney asked the woman victim in a rape case to point out her assailant, the woman on the witness stand pointed to me— much to the amusement of the judge, city attorney, court clerks, and bailiff.

"Luckily, however, the woman eventually realized her mistake and identified some other culprit, one of the men standing in the prisoner dock behind our press box.

"I sure hope she picked the right man," said the rotund Reddin. "He was rather tall and skinny, I recall."

Reddin and Jack Jarvis of the *P-I*, among others, used to sneak up to the top floor of the police building, where Seattle City Hospital was also located, and make ham-and-cheese sandwiches or get nurses to shampoo their hair. They and others would pool their money and send someone off to Chinatown for lottery tickets. They played poker with cops and had barbecues in the pressroom, using a pit they built from stolen bricks. Room 111 was the press space from 1909 until the building was closed in 1950, when manual typewriters were still the rage; everyone lugged their Royals and Underwood uprights up to a new Public Safety Building on Third Avenue, cop headquarters for the rest of the century. There the horseplay continued—*P-I* police reporter Bob Ward is still fondly remembered for stealing a police cruiser and driving around town whistling at women and dogs over the car's loudspeaker. Embellishment remained a newspaper staple as well. Vince O'Keefe, a *Times* police reporter who later became the paper's executive sports editor, recalled writing a story in the fifties about a man who committed suicide in his jail cell by chewing through his own wrist, flesh and bone. "If I remember correctly," O'Keefe recalled, "the headline actually said 'Man Bites Self to Death.'"

But vice in particular sold newspapers, and there was much of it to write about. Reporters often came to work optimistic that, before the day was over, they would be hunting-and-pecking about Nellie Curtis, for one. Operating out of Pike Place Market, Madam Nellie ran one of a dozen downtown bordellos in the fifties. During World War II, when Japanese Americans were forced out of their homes and businesses and interned at prison camps, Curtis had taken over one such family's lease at the 57-room Outlook Hotel, in the elbow of the market beneath the famous 1930 steroidal clock. She remodeled and renamed it the LaSalle, as it's still known, moved in with her vast collection of hats, and drew heavy-breathing, cash-waving throngs to her upstairs cribs. Back when Navy ships routinely tied up on Seattle's waterfront, sailors on some occasions created a noticeable line outside the LaSalle's front door.

To operate back then required paying off the cops on the beat and greasing the wheels at City Hall. It didn't much matter who was in charge, Curtis wrote in a letter to a relative about the 1948 mayoral election: "I have been at the same deal, with tougher ones and mean ones [politicians] and I am still in the same place doing the same, and I took my ups and downs, worse than at present and came out on top, so it doesn't matter to me who gets in, I will always find my own outs, and go as I am." And make an astonishing amount of money doing it. Sodeko Ikeda, who visited the LaSalle in the fifties to inquire about buying the building, recounted to historian Murray Morgan how Curtis couldn't find the door keys while looking through a series of drawers. "I saw a lot of money in every drawer she pulled out," Ikeda said. "She had a vanity and a dresser. She pulled out the lamp stand drawers, too. And in every drawer she pulled out she had a lot of cash. Some was lying flat, some was stacked up."

Still, Curtis was feeling increased heat in Seattle, and payoffs took an ever-larger bite of profits. She sold off the LaSalle in 1951, reopened a smaller operation at an old hotel down the street, and began scoping out ventures elsewhere. In 1952 she bought a hotel in Aberdeen, Washington, on the Pacific coast, where prostitution seemed to rival logging and lumber mills as an industry. There had been only one well-known whorehouse in the adjoining town of Hoquiam, above the old Sailor's Rest tavern. By the fifties, the building was so old it was leaning at a steep angle, and it eventually collapsed. As one local put it, "They fucked it down." But in Aberdeen, brothels were booming.

As the owner of the newly named Curtis Hotel, Nellie would become the logging community's most famed, if not infamous, figure, a legend that may still eclipse some later historic figures, including two Grays Harbor Nobel Prize winners—George Hitchings of Hoquiam (Physiology and Medicine, 1988) and Douglas Osheroff of Aberdeen (Physics, 1996)—but with the likely exception of a musician named Kurt Cobain.

Curtis had six women living and working full-time at her cathouse, as most Harborites called the downtown brothels that began expanding once Nellie set up shop. Curtis was the madam from Seattle who had found a friendly small town in need of an economic and sexual spurt—and an outlet for its wayward youths. Thanks in great deal to Nellie, any local teen growing up in the fifties could have sex with an older woman. He would need $5 and acceptable fake identification, which in those days meant merely tapping a finger on a greasy car engine and pressing out a print on a card labeled "ID." A good post-pubescent stubble usually cinched the deal. Few, however, got beyond the sanitizing, presex bathing the women gave by hand, washing a customer's privates with soap and water from a bedside pan. Ulp, sorry. Five dollars, kid.

The Aberdeen cathouses—at one point, more than a dozen in a town of eighteen thousand—were staffed by white women, except for one house, known casually as the Chocolate Shop. Locals knew, walking down the street, who the prostitutes were: the best-dressed and -coiffed ladies in town. The houses were typically hotels and a few small residences along Aberdeen's main streets. Most popular were Nellie's place, the Harbor Rooms, and the 405, a small house with its street numbers in large neon out front. That was code. Prostitution in Aberdeen was done much as it was in Seattle, under a tolerance policy, and while the harbor town was even more wide open, its city fathers weren't about to allow signs that said "Cathouse." So madams gassed up their addresses in lights, a tip-off to locals as well as to Fort Lewis GIs and a lot of truck drivers who were supposed to be hauling ass from Seattle to Portland.

Late *Seattle Times* columnist Don Hannula, an Aberdeen native, once recalled that when he was an innocent Catholic parochial-school boy of about twelve, he delivered orders from his father's fish market along the Wishkah River to some of those so-called rooming houses and hotels downtown. "I thought," he said, "hotel workers sure dressed funny. They ordered fish or oysters every Friday. I used to wonder if they were all Catholic." Hannula remembered that, as in Seattle, "Local law enforcement clearly was paid off—but never caught. Cops and cathouses were very cozy. Bronco Tesia [a barkeep and curator of the Aberdeen Historical Whorehouse Restoration Society] remembered: 'The madam at the Star Rooms had a little dog that kept running out when customers came in. She'd call the cops to look for her dog and bring it back.'"

Thanks in great deal to Nellie Curtis's influence, a memorable 1956 *Seattle Times* headline reported "Aberdeen 'Most Wide-Open City' in State, Law-Enforcers Declare." Mayor Ed Lundgren told *Times* reporters he was shocked to hear there were brothels in his town. It would be an even bigger shock, he added, if they were shut down.

They were, three years later, with a fed-up, Russian-born Aberdeen police captain named Nick Yantsin doing the honors, ending Nellie Curtis's hallowed career in the process. On January 31, 1959, accompanied by a Presbyterian minister, Yantsin and a small force of cops busted the Harbor Rooms and arrested eighteen men and five women. The town was never the same. Until then, Yantsin recalled, he'd bought into the tolerance policy, figuring it was a "necessary evil." Echoing the thinking in Seattle, Yantsin said, "The notion was that if you didn't have it, decent women and girls would be endangered by these lust-crazed loggers and all that sort of thing. And so it was tolerated. And I went right along with it." After the 1956 headlines and denials, which only generated more business for the houses, he eventually changed his mind and decided to "poke a hole in their hypocrisy."

The raid didn't have the mayor and City Council's blessings, however, and Yantsin was fired. Aberdeen was divided in its view of the crackdown. Some felt the town needed cleaning up, while others wondered what that might do to the economic base. The ladies of the evening spent their earnings at local stores and markets and brought in out-of-towners who put away a lot of food and booze. Yantsin's renegade raid hit people in their pocketbooks. Even his daughter, a popular high school cheerleader, was booed by fellow students. A writer for the school paper drew up an editorial supporting Yantsin, but it was spiked as too controversial.

In their book about Aberdeen, *On the Harbor: From Black Friday to Nirvana*, John C. Hughes and Ryan Teague Beckwith note that Curtis fought back against Yantsin, having *him* arrested. She was allowed to swear out a warrant accusing him of entering her hotel without permission, and she and Yantsin wound up facing off in court one day. She told a judge she merely ran a rooming house, where her "renters" lived, and there wasn't much else to it. The cop was trespassing.

Then Yantsin's attorney asked if she was a prostitute.

"I never was," Curtis answered.

"A madam?" he asked.

"Fifth Amendment," she said.

Later she was asked if she ever employed prostitutes, in Seattle say, and she again invoked her right not to incriminate herself. The case was dismissed.

Tolerance ultimately lost out to enforcing the law, and Captain Yantsin was reinstated—and even eventually named Aberdeen Cop of the Year. But the Harbor cathouse era was ending, smoldering for a few years until all the joints closed. Mayor Lundgren fell into some disrepute as well when it was reported that his construction company had been paid $10,000 by Nellie to remodel her hotel.

Curtis pulled up stakes in Aberdeen and was in the throes of shutting down her Seattle operation. She went to her home in West Seattle, a compound surrounded by a high steel fence along Alki Beach, and asked to be let alone. "After nearly half a century in the oldest profession in the world, Nellie Curtis had retired," write Hughes and Beckwith.

Within a few years, Curtis was charged with evading taxes on almost $173,000 in earnings. A list of her elite customers never surfaced, but she had some hoity-toity business partners. Court records showed Curtis had loaned $140,000 to Seattle furrier Milton Jones and had taken out two mortgages—which the IRS termed "false" transactions—worth $43,500 on her Aberdeen hotel with one of the heirs of the Friedlander & Sons jewelry chain of Seattle. Her tax tab, with penalties, exceeded $250,000. She was in court for years but, weakened by two heart attacks, Curtis settled with the IRS for $120,000 in 1971. She died five years later, at seventy-five. The following year, her

Stripper Gypsy Rose Lee, a Seattle native, back in town during a book tour for her memoirs in 1957. (Photo: *Seattle Post-Intelligencer* Collection, MOHAI)

companion, Martin Jansen, was killed in a gasoline-fueled fire at the Alki home. It was thought to be a suicide.

Curtis was the last chapter of memorable Northwest cathouse history—she reputedly ran a house in Centralia, too. The LaSalle, built in 1901 and renovated in recent years, is now affordable housing for seniors at Pike Place Market, but remains a curiosity for those who know its history. Down in Aberdeen, however, Nellie's past has been turned to rubble. As Don Hannula recalled in a column, Curtis's legend "hit rock bottom, when they turned the grandest cathouse in town—the Harbor Rooms—into a Jack in the Box."

In the sixties the last of Seattle's burlesque theaters was also in its waning days. The Rivoli at First Avenue and Madison Street was the only such strip show remaining. The Palace Hip, where Charlie Chaplin used to dance for $100 a week, had already folded at Second and Madison, where it had been opened in 1910 by theater pioneer John Considine. The Rivoli—born the Tivoli in 1913—had rocked on, still attracting great strippers, including Tempest Storm and Seattle-born Gypsy Rose Lee, whose sister was actress June Havoc.

Lee's strip career was coming to an end as well, though her fame continued with successful books and a musical about her life. She had been one of the biggest stars of Minsky's Burlesque and was frequently arrested in raids in Seattle and around the circuit. Dancers, it seemed, aroused the indignity, if not the libido, of cops by not only stripping down to G-strings and pasties, but sometimes even taking them off! After watching the full performance in the line of duty, cops rushed the dressing rooms and dispatched the arrested performers to the waiting paddy wagons. They were usually back in time for the next day's performance, if the proper payoff had been made.

The Rivoli Theatre on 1st Avenue, circa 1950. The establishment was also know as the Gayety, Star Oak, and Rivoli Garden. (Photo: Museum of History & Industry)

Stripper Candy Renee ran for a Seattle precinct committeewoman position in 1957. (Photo: *Seattle Post-Intelligencer* Collection, MOHAI)

Seattle was an important stop on the strip circuit, and Lee helped make it so. As a performer she was so seductive and funny that legendary writer H. L. Mencken was moved to coin a term in honor of her high-class style: ecdysiast—striptease artist. Lee wrote a novel, called *The G-String Murders*, that was later made into the film *Lady of Burlesque*, starring Barbara Stanwyck. She produced a memoir, *Gypsy*, as well. Throughout her life, she had a stormy relationship with her mother, Rose, who had once tried to shoot sister June's husband. The gun's safety was on, giving him time to flee. Mother Rose died of cancer, and when Lee discovered she, too, had cancer, she told June, "This is my present, you know, my present from mother." Lee died in 1970, as did the Rivoli, which had become a porn theater. It was turned into a parking garage, then torn down and replaced by a high-rise.

Also among the Rivoli's strippers was a performer named Candy Renee, who claimed to be a staunch Republican. In 1956, as a stunt, she filed for political office in Seattle to see "everyone get a fair shake." Though it was merely a precinct committeewoman position, she claimed she was also considering running for the Legislature. She hoped to spur a repeal of the state's blue laws, which limited bar hours and prevented liquor sales on Sundays. "Any man who can find fault with my platform is plainly closing his eyes to the facts," she said, hand on curvy hip.

Portland police took interest in her candidacy as well. They wanted to question her in connection with an emerging Rose City vice and payoff scandal. Renee had once been found with drugs and a gun in her car, and had dated a Portland cop. According to a state police report, she said she didn't know about any payoffs; as for the cop, she dated him because, "like any other woman, [I] liked to be laid once in awhile." That scandal was about to break and would ultimately resonate to Seattle.

So would another scandal, in Tacoma, where a future governor was vowing to clean up civic corruption.

The Aroma of Tacoma

**Amanda Truelove said the city commissioner became
"polluted and fell from a sofa."**

State senator Albert Rosellini, a self-styled law-and-order
politico, said he'd heard enough about the corruption and
racketeering in Tacoma, the City of Destiny, and its underworld
links to Seattle. By Thanksgiving 1951, he had assembled a state
inquiry panel for weeklong hearings at the Tacoma Armory. The
intention was to get to the bottom of entrenched payoffs—and
perhaps boost his chances of becoming governor. Both worked
out, thanks in part to a live broadcast of the hearings in black-
and-white on Seattle's KING-TV. It was the first time the station
had telecast from the astonishing distance of thirty miles.

The tone was set by some of the early witnesses. The
Reverend Harold B. Long, pastor of the Immanuel Presbyterian
Church, opened his Bible to refresh himself, then opined that
"vice conditions here stemmed from the love of money, the root
of all evil." Mrs. Delbert Gundstrom, noted clubwoman, said
her life had been threatened over the phone because she was leading an effort to recall one of the suspected corrupt city officials.

She also testified that marijuana was available in Tacoma. Why, even young people were smoking it!

City prosecutor—later state attorney general and gubernatorial candidate—John J. O'Connell said he'd determined that Tacoma cops were collecting $20,000 a month in payoffs. Mrs. Eddie Morgan said her husband, a car salesman, had committed suicide after losing $5,000 in three days to a bookie on Commerce Street. Retired policeman Don Davies testified that a local radio personality, Burt McMurtrie, had been beaten up by local vigilantes after criticizing the police administration. Even then-radio commentator and historian Murray Morgan said he'd been threatened for speaking out.

One of the local pinball kings, Vito Cuttone, said he made a fortune but insisted he never made payoffs, and denied he offered $50,000 to a local minister if his church would back Cuttone's favorite politicians in the next election. Another pinball operator said he was paying off at $50 a month. More than a dozen others took their places on the witness stand, telling of payoffs to permit gambling, and of kickbacks on towing contracts.

Perhaps most memorable was the testimony of Lil Buckeley, better known as "Amanda Truelove," a self-confessed bootlegger. She claimed that two top Tacoma officials, including city safety commissioner James Kerr, were present at a City Hall conference where it was agreed her monthly payoff to the cops would be dropped from $1,000 down to $800. Truelove said Kerr also visited her at the Union Hotel where, after downing strong doses of whiskey from miniature bottles, he became "polluted and fell from a sofa."

Alma Jackson, a black Tacoma madam who'd been reluctant to testify for fear of her life, finally showed up and named the cops she paid bribes to, in cash, whiskey, and women. She also said she paid $800 to a man named Harry Hoffman. In subsequent years, he would be accused of bribing Seattle cops with the help of Frank Colacurcio.

Frank's name didn't come up then, perhaps to the liking of his former attorney. Afterward, Rosellini said he felt some Tacomans were lying under oath, and that perjury charges were in order. Tacoma's police chief Jack Elich promised an all-out investigation of payoffs.

But there it ended. The minimal effect was to slow the vice action in Tacoma and expand the market for it up Highway 99. Both pinball and slot machines were illegal in Seattle, yet could be found in bars and private clubs. Though laws banning slots and pinballs had been passed and upheld by the Washington Supreme Court, and a ban was supposedly being enforced by King County prosecutor Charles O. "Chuck" Carroll and Sheriff Harlan S. Callahan, the Seattle action continued, interrupted now and then by a brief crackdown and quick comeback. A legislative bill was introduced in 1953 to legalize slot machines statewide in private clubs; it failed in the House by a single vote. Playing continued anyway. The Seattle City Council also passed an ordinance that, in defiance of state law, licensed local card rooms. It was done under the tolerance policy theory of controlling sin by bringing it into the open. That effectively legitimized graft, opening the door to payoffs by allowing street-level vice and patrol officers to regulate criminal operations. Cops could extort from operators, demanding they pay to play, while City Hall averted its eyes and put out its hand, collecting license revenues. Liquor inspectors got in on the take, too, suspending licenses of bar owners who refused to pay bribes.

As the action in both Tacoma and Seattle indicated, public officials accepted tolerance as a creative way to do things. It was

Pinball machines used to pay cash prizes, but that became illegal in the early 1960s. (Photo: *Seattle Post-Intelligencer* Collection, MOHAI)

no secret that operators were skirting the law, although details of the extensive, growing payoff system weren't yet being exposed on the front pages. Besides, local and state governments were cashing in, as were individual public officials. In the late fifties there were almost 5,800 pinball, slot, and other illegal gambling devices operating in Washington. It's something the state clearly knew because it was taxing each device on 20 percent of the gross take. Most were pinball machines, operating in just about every county of the state, said Charles Hodde, a tax commission member. The list included twenty-seven slot machines, which were being taxed at 40 percent of their take.

It was a bit ambiguous. Did the state have laws or didn't it? By never strictly defining and enforcing the rules under which people could be arrested, the government created an atmosphere for abuse. Cops were given wide berth in deciding which laws they would enforce—or break.

In this climate of crookedness, anything seemed possible. Take the events surrounding the sixtieth annual Seattle Policeman's Ball, in 1954.

The drunken bacchanalia was roaring away at a downtown ballroom when, a few blocks up the street, burglars began breaking into the Pioneer Safe Deposit Vaults at 701 First Avenue. It was the start of the three-day Washington's Birthday weekend. Using lanterns, footlockers of tools, and weighty drilling equipment, the thieves sealed up the building from light and sound, then cut through steel doors and broke down a brick wall. With acetylene cutting torches, they burned the vault wall for hours until it melted. They opened just 416 of the 1,640 boxes and compartments. As the cops danced, the crooks waltzed out the door. The take was reputedly a few hundred thousand dollars. Others later said it was half a million. It has reached a legendary $1 million in today's retellings, remaining perhaps the biggest unsolved bank job in Seattle history. (That heist has a rival, however: in 1998 burglars drilled through the eighteen-inch-thick vault ceiling of the Chinatown/International District branch of Key Bank and made off with at least $500,000, but possibly up to $1 million.)

Pioneer Vaults manager Frank Goodman discovered the loss the following week and called in police, who quickly theorized the burglary was undertaken by at least three men, with a fourth posted as a lookout. One detective told reporters the thieves "were highly skilled operators, a type from which Seattle has been free for several years." But no one was ever nabbed, and the only trace of the loot was a single stolen bond that later turned up in Nevada. Anyone who recounted the heist back then usually ended their story with, "So, wouldn't the cops have to be in on it?" Recalls Seattle's HistoryLink.org:

> Some cynics supposed the vaults were used by corrupt city officials to hide caches of "dirty" money, and inside knowledge of the vaults, the perfect timing and flawless execution of the burglary suggested police involvement.

Christopher Bayley, a Seattle attorney who became a reform prosecutor in the seventies, felt Seattle's history of widespread police corruption was rooted in tolerance-policy thinking. But the policy was "a seemingly virtuous impulse" to control low-level vice, he said, which not surprisingly created more vice and crime. State and local laws dating to Prohibition had kept bars closed on Sundays, and legal gambling had been limited to low-stakes card rooms and charity bingo games, at least on the surface. "Those laws conflicted with the climate of a port city, where citizens and visitors alike wanted to drink and gamble," Bayley said. Over time, the city developed its unwritten policy. "Bars and clubs could break the rules—for a price. Local beat cops, vice detectives and, ultimately, local officials profited by accepting payoffs from businesses in return for ignoring illegal or after-hours drinking and gambling." It was a tacit policy to enforce the law by breaking it.

And that was music to the Colacurcio Bros. Amusement Co.

Goon Squad

"Colacurcio implied that if I did not stop talking to these
persons, I or one of my family would be physically injured."

By the fifties, Frank Colacurcio and his farming brothers had
turned their attention to vice as a profession. They gave up
produce and took up gambling. Frank's brother Bill obtained a
city amusement license and went into the coin-operated machine
business. He established a small pinball route, servicing and
delivering machines to a few bars. He worked independently, at
first opposing the Amusement Owners Association of Seattle, the
industry group he refused to join. The Colacurcio Bros. Amusement Co.—Bill, Frank, and Sam—leased out jukebox and pinball machines. They also distributed cigarette- and food-vending
machines. Over the next five years, their business soared at clubs,
bars, and restaurants. The competition for locations was cut-
throat; the Colacurcios rose to the occasion, and into the sights
of vice investigators. The papers dubbed Bill, who came to claim
more than 135 machine licenses, the Pinball King. Frank, with
three dozen music locations, became the Jukebox King.

The talk was that Frank offered bar operators two business plans: lease his jukebox and he could fix your problems with the state Liquor Control Board; don't lease his jukebox and he could fix you. By the late fifties Frank's supposed liquor board influence and problem solving, particularly at the rowdy bars on First Avenue, had become part of an ongoing probe into jukebox racketeering. Operators said they'd been threatened and some of their equipment damaged. They pointed the finger at the Colacurcios. By the end of the year, Frank was busted by the cops after four businessmen swore he had threatened them with bodily harm.

One of the complainants, Ralph Alger, owner of the rival Hi-Tone Music Co., was worried enough about the threats to get out of the business, selling his jukebox concession at $25,000 less than he was offered a year earlier. In a matter of months, he had lost a half-dozen music locations to the Colacurcio Bros. and claimed his ex-customers were too frightened to tell him why they had switched. Alger said he went to Ciro's restaurant on Pine, run by two of Frank's sisters, and left a message for Frank to stop using "unfair tactics." A week later, Frank told him to quit harassing his customers.

"Colacurcio implied that if I did not stop talking to these persons, I or one of my family would be physically injured," said Alger. Another operator, John Chigaras, owner of Apollo Amusement Co., said Frank told him to back off or he'd be "found in an alley somewhere." Frank said they had it all wrong. He'd been in the business only six months, he told a reporter, with thirty-five locations he obtained "through friendship or promise of better service" or via the influence of brother Bill. He wasn't threatening anyone, Frank said, and in fact it was he who was being "pushed around."

In a 1958 trial for making threats, Frank heard four rivals or ex-customers recall his intimidating sales tactics. "I'm going

to stomp you in the street," is how First Avenue tavern owner
Bill Petro recalled Frank's pitch after Petro replaced Frank's
jukebox with a rival's. "He called me vile names and asked
me out in the street. I didn't go. I heard a lot of hearsay that
he might beat me up or have me beaten up." Harold Arnold,
owner of the Union Café, testified he offered Colacurcio a
partnership in a restaurant and lounge he was planning after
Frank said he could grease the licensing process with the liquor
board. When the license application fell through, he had
Colacurcio remove his music machine. He, too, was invited
into the street, he said, but passed. Were you afraid of Frank,
who was five foot seven and a solid 210 pounds, Arnold was
asked. "Personally," said the five foot ten, 150-pound Arnold,
"I [did] have a little fear about it—yes." Colacurcio was sitting
in the court's front row at the time, smiling thinly. Chigaras,
the Apollo Amusement owner, was also asked if he was afraid
of Frank and his crew. "I don't know—it looks like a goon
squad to me," he said. Jukebox distributor Alger, the rival who
ended up selling his business, said Frank had told him to "lay
off" in his attempts to compete with the Colacurcio brothers. "He may not hurt you," Alger said of Frank's threatening
ways, "but he can get you hurt."

A prosecutor said another witness who had planned to testify was now refusing, explaining he'd "rather leave the state
than be shot." But in the odd ways of justice then, a judge
found the testimony by Petro and the others truthful, yet
merely ordered Colacurcio to post a $5,000 peace bond. It
required him to be good for six months or go to jail. He was
otherwise free to go.

Within six hours he was back in court—with a lawsuit, suing his accusers for defamation, seeking $300,000
in damages. The suit claimed the bar and amusement

operators were trying to put Frank out of business by falsely accusing him of being a gangster, claiming he'd established a criminal syndicate that used force, coercion, and duress to take over the local jukebox industry. He said they also implied he carried a weapon and was a political boss.

The suit never went anywhere. But it generated headlines that, unfortunately for Frank, tended to reinforce in print and the public record just what he was denying, that Frank was a mobster.

Brother Bill also fell under investigation for his tactics in the pinball business. Only months after his brother's jukebox trial, Bill's eleven-year city license was facing revocation by City Hall. Responding to public insistence that something be done about the growing corruption, the council froze existing pinball and jukebox licenses and weighed changes in the law. The notion was to throw more light on who operators were by imposing full-disclosure clauses, requiring businesses to list investors or anyone with financial interests. Of sixty-three pinball franchise renewals put on hold, the council then took action on just one: Bill Colacurcio's. They voted unanimously against renewing his license. The decision was officially based on Bill's minor arrest record—a $100 fine for gambling (he wasn't prosecuted in another case, a paternity matter that had been settled quietly). But it was obviously a decision motivated by the amusement company's reputation.

The newspapers almost immediately changed Bill's title to the "Deposed" Pinball King of Seattle. But he and Frank still had their music business, for the moment.

Bobby Kennedy Calling

Amusement business? "What does that mean?
Does he have an orchestra, or what?"

By 1959 Bill and Frank were facing new laws to control jukebox licenses as well. Among the measures was a competition-limiting "bumping" rule, which prevented license holders from bumping a competitor's jukebox from a business without the businessman's clear approval. The law was obviously aimed at crippling Frank's strong-arm tactics.

Bill denied his brother was his enforcer and said they'd become successful by throwing solid pitches rather than punches. But those tactics, undercutting their rivals, also came under fire; giving away free music and other perks to customers appeared to break city amusement codes. Bill's lawyer accused the City Council and cops of "trying to deprive a man of a $50,000 to $100,000 a year business on a technicality."

Frank's widening reputation, however, was causing larger problems—problems that were suddenly reaching all the way to the other Washington. The crime boss role he denied in that 1958 lawsuit had come to the attention of the Senate labor racketeering committee, as part of a history-making investigation into the Teamsters union. Bobby Kennedy wanted to chat about it with Frank.

The *Seattle Times* reported in February 1959 that "Colacurcio, 41, is the only person from the Pacific Northwest summoned . . . Robert F. Kennedy, committee counsel, said the hearings will delve into ownership and distribution of music and pinball machines and will disclose racketeering," much of it swirling around the corrupt activities of the Teamsters, led by Seattle-born union boss Dave Beck, who was suspected of siphoning off Teamster funds for personal use and political payoffs.

The *Times* story was written by Ed Guthman, who won a Pulitzer Prize in 1950 for a series that exonerated University of Washington professor Melvin Rader, wrongly accused of being a Communist. Two years after he wrote about Kennedy's probe of Colacurcio, Guthman left the *Times* to work as press secretary for Kennedy, who became attorney general following the election of his brother John F. Kennedy in 1960. (Guthman wrote or coedited four books about Bobby Kennedy, but said his most satisfying career moment was being named to Richard Nixon's infamous "enemies list.")

Colacurcio told Guthman that Kennedy was wasting his time—Frank was already out of the music business, he said. He had sold his interests to his brother. "I'm looking for something to do," he said. "I don't know why I've been subpoenaed. If it is about that music-machine deal last year when I was rousted around, I'm not worried. We never did anything that wasn't ethical."

Frank had come to the committee's attention during the earlier testimony of Portland mobster James Elkins. "Big Jim" was summoned and agreeably testified in 1957 before the

Robert F. Kennedy, then a Washington, D.C., attorney, in Seattle during the U.S. Senate committee hearings on organized crime. Kennedy
was the committee's chief counsel. (Photo: *Seattle Post-Intelligencer*
Collection, MOHAI)

committee—officially, the Senate Select Committee on Improper Activities in the Labor or Management Field, and unofficially, the McClellan Committee, named for its chair, Arkansas Democrat John McClellan. The committee included three future presidential candidates, Bobby and Jack Kennedy and Barry Goldwater, and one ruthless Commie hunter, Joe McCarthy (who would later would fall from grace with the help of Edward R. Murrow, the legendary CBS broadcaster raised in Skagit County). The committee's main targets were Jimmy Hoffa and his predecessor Beck, the former Broadway High School student and Seattle laundry truck driver who rose through the Teamsters ranks and was elected its president in 1952.

Beck had been one of the first to appear before the committee, and Bobby Kennedy went at him, wanting to know what happened to $322,000 missing from the union's treasury. Beck wasn't saying. He was barely speaking. To 117 questions, he invoked his Fifth Amendment right not to answer.

The hearings, which were spread out over two years, initially focused on reports that Teamsters were trying to take over the rackets in Portland. History seems to have mostly overlooked the committee's exposure of the Teamsters' corrosive role in Seattle vice and political corruption, however. While considered a probe of Portland's rackets, the hearings, in retrospect, revealed as much or more about Seattle's criminal underbelly and how the union worked in concert with Frank and others to control it. Under Beck, the Seattle Teamsters allied themselves with bars and card rooms, pinball operators and bingo parlors, madams and prostitutes. They could control much of the commerce because they drove the delivery trucks. Businesses that didn't go along got visits from the archetypical Teamster—size twenty neck, size five hat—who, in addition to making threats, would start fights and cause disturbances. Rather than working for employers, the Teamsters became *their* bosses.

One of Beck's vice presidents, Seattle Teamster Frank Brewster, was reported to be leader of the union goon squad that got things done under Beck's rule. A 1945 General Crime Survey Report, compiled by FBI officials in Seattle, had claimed Brewster controlled a Seattle crime syndicate and used money and muscle to influence Seattle political leaders and vice cops. According to historian Robert C. Donnelly, "Brewster had developed a business and personal relationship with Seattle and Spokane vice racketeer Thomas Maloney, a relationship built on real estate and organized crime. The FBI uncovered evidence that Maloney, an established gambler and prostitute broker and an associate of the Frank Colacurcio crime family, and Joe McLaughlin, a Seattle crime figure and close friend of Brewster, were on Teamsters payrolls. Brewster also reportedly arranged for Maloney to receive a loan from Local 690 to bail out his Spokane restaurant and gambling operation."

In 1956, Portland's major newspaper, the *Oregonian*, first had the story. Under the headline "City, County Control Sought by Gangsters," investigative reporters Wally Turner and William Lambert detailed the failed Seattle takeover of Portland's vice industry. It was the start of a series that would go on to win that year's Pulitzer Prize for local reporting (Lambert went on to work for *LIFE* magazine, where he disclosed how U.S. Supreme Court Justice Abe Fortas had accepted a questionable $20,000 fee, leading to his resignation; Turner joined the *New York Times* and ended his career as its bureau chief in Seattle in the eighties).

Writes Donnelly: "The Seattle group's plan to take over Portland's lucrative vice industry began to unravel. The business relationship among James Elkins, corrupt Teamsters officials, and the Seattle racketeers ended when, according to Elkins, Thomas Maloney suggested opening three or four houses of prostitution and establishing an abortion ring. Maloney arranged a meeting between Elkins and Ann Thompson, a successful Seattle madam. . . . Soon after, Maloney arranged for a meeting between Elkins and Seattle vice operator Frank Colacurcio."

As detailed transcripts of the committee hearings show, Elkins told Kennedy the powerful Seattle union bosses were going to move into Portland's vice trade and needed people who'd been instrumental in Seattle's corrupt payoff system.

> Kennedy: What type of things did they [Teamsters] want to get open?
>
> Elkins: Horse book, punch board, pinballs, houses.
>
> Kennedy: Was there more discussion at that time about houses of prostitution?
>
> Elkins: A little discussion, yes, I think on one or two occasions.

So you talked with the Teamsters, Kennedy said during the 1957 questioning. Did they bring anybody else down from Seattle? "Yes," said Elkins, "they brought Frank Colacurcio down."

Who, Kennedy asked, was Frank Colacurcio?

> Elkins: Well, I knew him to be another racketeer.
>
> Kennedy: A racketeer?
>
> Elkins: Yes . . .
>
> Kennedy: Did you have a meeting with Frank Colacurcio?
>
> Elkins: Yes, sir.
>
> Kennedy: Where did you have a meeting with him?

Elkins: In Tom and Joe's apartment, Tom Maloney and Joe McLaughlin's apartment in Portland Towers.

Kennedy: That was Frank Colacurcio?

Elkins: He was a boy that had various things operating in Seattle.

Kennedy: He was in the same kind of business as you, but more.

Elkins: That is right.

Kennedy: And he was operating in Seattle?

Elkins: And Washington, yes.

Kennedy: In the State of Washington?

Elkins: That is right.

Kennedy: What conversations and discussions did you have with Frank Colacurcio when he came down to Portland?

Elkins: He wanted me to arrange so that he could take over three or four houses. I told him if he wanted the houses to go buy them.

Chairman: What kind of houses?

Elkins: Rooming houses for houses of prostitution, sir.

Chairman: All right.

Kennedy: What other conversation did you have with him about them?

Elkins: It wound up in a row.

Kennedy: For what reason?

Elkins: Well, he said he would pay for them out of the earning of them and I said I didn't think that they would run long enough for that.

Kennedy: Why did you say that?

Elkins: Because I was telling him the truth. I didn't think they would run; I thought they would get arrested.

Kennedy: So you didn't reach any agreement with Colacurcio?

Elkins: No, I did not.

Kennedy: He went back.

Elkins: That is correct.

At the time, Elkins was among those snared in a vice crackdown following the *Oregonian* stories and was under indictment—one of 115 indictments handed down by three different Portland grand juries in 1956 and 1957. To Kennedy and the committee, he was a seemingly candid witness, even if he lied from time to time (he denied he had anything to do with prostitution, for example, but his record shows he had worked as a pimp and married two of his girls).

Elkins said he needed labor's blessing to place his pinball machines in some Portland locations. He was put in touch with Seattle racetrack and gambling figure Maloney, who was close to Brewster and Portland Teamster leader John Sweeney, who would later become a Seattle Teamster bigwig.

It turned out that, while Elkins wanted Maloney's help with the union in Portland, Maloney wanted Elkins's assistance with the cops in Seattle.

Say what? Kennedy asked Elkins.

Elkins: Well, he [Maloney] wanted to open up one gambling and bootleg place in Seattle, in partners with someone. I don't believe he said who. Maybe it was a colored person. He asked me to speak to an official that I knew of there.

Kennedy: He asked you to speak to the [Seattle] chief of police?

Elkins: That is right.

Kennedy: Did you speak to the chief of police?

Elkins: I did. But I don't want to give any idea that I ever give him any money, because I haven't.

Kennedy. But you spoke to the chief of police?

Elkins: That is right.

Kennedy: The chief of police, what did he say about Tom Maloney?

Elkins: He said . . . he would see what he could do.

Kennedy: He allowed them to open one place?

Elkins: He either allowed it or arranged for him to open one, yes.

Kennedy: Did you later learn that Tom Maloney turned around and opened two places?

Elkins: I believe that either he or someone else told me that he opened one, and wanted to run the town or something, and he closed that place.

Kennedy: The chief of police to whom you spoke then closed both of the places down?

Elkins: That is right.

Kennedy: With the understanding or feeling that Tom Maloney had overstepped his bounds going into the second place?

Elkins: Yes.

Later, Kennedy asked more about a 1955 Seattle meeting with Maloney and Portland district attorney William Langley.

Kennedy: You came up and met Tom Maloney and William Langley at the Olympic Hotel.

Elkins: Yes.

Kennedy: In a room at the hotel and will you tell the committee what went on in that hotel room?

Elkins: Well, I asked what is the purpose of the meeting and they said it is just a discussion about what we are going to do. . . . They said they were going to have a discussion about what was going to take place when Langley went in, and I said, "In what way?" "Well," he said, "you are going to have a little gambling and a little this and a little that."

Kennedy: What is a little of this and a little of that?

Elkins: Card rooms, horse books, and I think he mentioned three or four houses of prostitution, bootlegging joints, punchboards.

Kennedy: Who said this to you?

Elkins: Bill said, "We are going to discuss what is going to go."

Kennedy: Bill is Bill Langley?

Elkins: Bill Langley.

Kennedy: He was the newly elected district attorney?

Elkins: Yes, that is correct.

Kennedy: And he was telling you what was to be allowed to go in the city?

Elkins: That is right. He said, "I want Tom in the picture. I am going to cut my take with him until he gets going."

Kennedy: What did he mean by that?

Elkins: Well, what the payoff was to him, he told me that he had to split it with Tom . . .

Kennedy: Now, what did you say when Langley suggested opening three or four houses of prostitution? . . . Was that actually suggested by Maloney or was it suggested by Langley?

Elkins: It was suggested by Maloney. . . . He said "It is okay with Bill for three or four houses and I am going to take you down and introduce you to Ann Thompson."

Kennedy: And who was Ann Thompson?

Elkins: Well, according to Tom—I didn't know her—she was a professional madam.

Kennedy: And what did he say about her?

Elkins: Well, he wanted to introduce me and he said he wanted her to supervise the houses . . .

Kennedy: When was the next meeting?

Elkins: In three or four days John Sweeney called me and told me to come to Seattle in the next day or two and so I went up.

Kennedy: John Sweeney is now up in Seattle?

Elkins: John Sweeney is dead.

Kennedy: But I mean he was up at Seattle and Clyde Crosby replaced him in Portland.

Elkins: That is right. So I went to the Teamsters hall in Seattle and Joe McLaughlin meets me in the hall and he takes me into a room and John Sweeney, Tom Maloney, and Joe McLaughlin and another man was in there, who they introduced me to, but I couldn't swear what his name is right now. Sweeney said "He is one of the boys and you can talk freely in front of him." They talked about pinballs and punchboards and then he told me "I want you to sit down with Tom" . . .

Kennedy: Was there any discussion about how the Teamsters or the Teamster union would help?

Elkins: That is correct. They said with the power of the Teamsters, and their weight behind it—Portland was not an open town and that the chief of police wouldn't go along with an open town—and they said either he will go along or the Teamsters will get him moved, meaning the chief of police.

Kennedy: They were going to get the chief of police moved?

Elkins: If he didn't go along. But they thought I was lying to them even at that time and they thought that I was operating under protection.

Kennedy: But they told you that they would have the help and assistance of the Teamster officials in Portland?

Elkins: That is correct.

Kennedy: And that [Seattle Teamsters] Frank Brewster and John Sweeney were behind this operation?

Elkins: That is right.

Later on, Kennedy asked Elkins about the role of Seattle madam Ann Thompson, whom Elkins went to see after she checked into a Portland hotel.

Kennedy: And what was discussed at that time?

Elkins: The minute I walked in the room she said "Just take it easy. I am not trying to get you to change your mind. I don't want to operate. But I want you to tell Maloney and his people that I was here and talked to you, but we couldn't get together," I believe is what she said, as near as I can remember. That might not be word for word, but that was the gist of it. She again repeated that she couldn't operate one or two or three places on the small percentage she would get. If she had a whole hatful of places, she probably could make a dollar.

Kennedy: So she wasn't very interested in it?

Elkins: She was not. . . .

Kennedy: You have not seen her since that time?

Elkins: No, I have not.

As Elkins stepped from the stand, Ann Thompson dramatically stood up in the hearing room. Tall and saucy, she was nonetheless shy, and held her big black purse to her face, saying, "No picture." As she walked to the stand, Kennedy announced, "The witness does not want her picture taken." Chairman McClellan beckoned to her. "Have a seat. You may be sworn first," he said, and then he addressed the cameramen in the photo gallery: "The photographers will not take any pictures until the chair gives you permission to do so."

Thompson, "dressed to the nines," as press reports put it back then, was sworn in but had little to tell the committee, essentially confirming Elkins's story. She was doing a good business bedding the men of Seattle and Tacoma, she indicated, while Portland looked like a money loser, even with the Teamsters along for the ride. Maloney had put her in touch with Elkins, so she felt they should at least talk.

> Kennedy: Does it seem strange to you that if Mr. Maloney fixed an appointment up with Elkins, on the assumption that Elkins wanted you to come down, that when you had your first conversation with him he discouraged you?
>
> Thompson: I will tell you, at the time I guess I was too much of an eager beaver . . .
>
> Kennedy: You had a pretty good reputation in the state of Washington for running these homes.
>
> Thompson: Thank you.

At a later senate hearing, in March 1957, Brewster, the Seattle Teamster, showed up to defend his union and himself, but gave up a lot of ground in the process. He confirmed his relationship with one of the Colacurcio brothers' pinball rivals, Fred Galeno.

Kennedy: Who is Fred Galeno?

Brewster: Fred Galeno is a person that is in Seattle, Washington.

Kennedy: What do you mean, a person in Seattle, Washington?

Brewster: Well . . . who is he—he is a person.

Kennedy: Is he in business in Seattle?

Brewster: Yes, he has a business.

Kennedy: What is his business?

Brewster: It is an amusement business.

Kennedy: What does that mean? Does he have an orchestra, or what? . . .

Brewster: He is in the amusement business that includes juke-boxes and pinballs.

Kennedy: He is in the pinball business?

Brewster: Yes. He is one of the oldest—one of the members of the oldest families in the city of Seattle.

The Teamster boss told how the union spent a lot of cash they didn't keep records on, almost impulsively doling it out to political candidates. Kennedy asked Brewster about one $4,000 allotment.

Kennedy: How was that to be spent, that $4,000?

Brewster: To be spent on candidates. [Teamster official] C. O'Reilly was in full charge, authorized by the executive board.

Kennedy: Is there anything in your books to indicate to whom that money went?

Brewster: No, there isn't. . . .

Kennedy: What would prevent Frank Brewster taking the $4,000 and using it to purchase or pay for some of his personal bills?

Brewster: That never was the purpose. . . .

Well, Kennedy wanted to know, where was this fund, this "special fund" for politics, located? The committee had traced much of the money from Local 174, which had been headed by Brewster. Supposedly earmarked for political campaigns, the total came to precisely $99,999.65 for just the 1952 elections. Where, exactly, had that money been kept, and to whom did it flow? Brewster couldn't say. The admission seemed to surprise Chairman McClellan, who stepped in with his own questions, as did senator Karl Mundt of South Dakota.

McClellan: This sounds like a lot of money for working people. Do you mean you cannot give any accounting of this money, where it went?

Brewster: That was handled by Claude O'Reilly.

McClellan: I know, but you were secretary and treasurer. You are supposed to know where it goes. Do you mean to say you did not know?

Brewster: I did not know.

Kennedy: I might say, Claude O'Reilly is dead now, is that right?

Brewster: Yes, he is dead now.

Mundt: Is it your position, Mr. Brewster, that all $99,000 of this was spent for political purposes in Seattle?

Brewster: And the state of Washington.

Mundt: $99,000, that is just in one campaign year, I presume, 1951 to 1953. You spent $99,000 in the state of Washington for political purposes in the campaign of 1952?

Brewster: It sounds like a big figure, but spread over everyone that knocks on your door, it isn't too much.

Mundt: Do you support everybody who knocks at your door?

Brewster: Most everyone. We ride a couple of horses in the race once in awhile.

Kennedy later steered the questioning toward the Seattle-Portland vice connection, and Brewster was quick to defend his old buddy and Teamster leader Sweeney: he had been maligned by the hearings, where "any hoodlum," Brewster said, "who chooses can get up and say 'John J. Sweeney did this,' and 'John J. Sweeney did that,' without fear of successful contradiction."

Well, what about you, then? Kennedy said, regarding "that talk or discussion you had with Jim Elkins in your office. . . . Did you say anything to him about the fact that he would be wading across Lake Washington in concrete boots, or anything like that?"

"I never said that to him or anyone in my life," Brewster said.

Kennedy then asked about the shadowy Maloney, the Portland-Seattle go-between. Brewster said there was nothing to it. The Teamsters had loaned him money to start up a Seattle card room, which Brewster didn't consider to be gambling. "They play a certain kind of cards," he said. "I don't think they play poker." (They did.)

He also didn't know that Maloney—for whom Brewster got a job at a racetrack—was a bookie. Actually, Brewster said, though he'd known Maloney two decades, he didn't know him that well. Kennedy should really be asking Sweeney, another dead guy, about that.

> Kennedy: You see the difficult position that it puts the committee in. [Maloney] had this history of twenty years of friendship with you, and you signed the checks to pay his bills down in Portland, you and John J. Sweeney . . . and then you come before the committee and say that it is all John J. Sweeney's responsibility, that it is his fault. And John J. Sweeney is dead so we cannot ask him about it. You see that that is a little difficult to understand.

> Brewster: Well, it might be for you, but it is not for me.

The televised hearings were watched by 1.2 million American households as the panel probed Teamsters' misuse of union funds and its ties to labor racketeers and organized crime. Only a handful of the more than one hundred people indicted in the Portland scandal were ever convicted, though they did include District Attorney Langley, who got off with a $428 fine for refusing to prosecute gamblers. Elkins was also convicted—of illegal wiretapping, having secretly recorded some of his conversations with the Teamsters. But the conviction was later overturned.

More than twenty Teamsters were convicted in subsequent criminal cases, including Jimmy Hoffa, found guilty of jury tampering in connection with an attempt to bribe a McClellan Committee investigator. After a long appeal, he went to prison for four years, was eventually pardoned by Richard Nixon, and quit the union. He was last seen in 1975 being driven away from Machus Red Fox restaurant in suburban Detroit, where he was planning to meet two Mafia leaders. Most versions of his final departure place him inside an oil drum, in which he was possibly cremated and/or buried within the fresh concrete of

Dave Beck, a leader of the Teamsters on the West Coast, being pulled away from reporters by his son, March 1957. (Photo: *Seattle Post-Intelligencer* Collection, MOHAI)

New Jersey's since demolished Giants Stadium. But he has also been reported to be, wholly or in part, in the Florida Everglades, a New Jersey Sanitation shredder or landfill, and an assortment of freshly laid East Coast freeways, buildings, and bridges.

Under pressure, Dave Beck opted not to run again for Teamsters president. In 1959 he was convicted of Washington state corruption charges for pocketing $1,900 he'd gotten from the sale of his union-owned Cadillac and separately was found guilty of six counts of federal income tax evasion. A federal sentencing judge, George Boldt, said as Beck stood before him: "No bootblack or newsboy of Horatio Alger's imagination ever rose from a more humble beginning to a greater height than Dave Beck." But "the exposure of Mr. Beck's insatiable greed, resulting in this fall from high place, is a sad and shocking story that cannot be contemplated by anyone with the slightest pleasure or satisfaction."

Beck went to prison for three years in 1962, but he turned out to be not quite the defeated man described by Boldt. Once free, he lived off his $50,000 Teamsters pension, invested in parking lots, and became a multimillionaire. He died in 1993, at age ninety-nine.

He went to his grave absolved of the grand larceny conviction for selling the Caddy. It was wiped away in 1965 with a pardon from Frank Colacurcio's former attorney, Governor Al Rosellini.

Sex and Car Bombshells

"I seen the belly dancers and what they were doing and
whatnot. That's how it became this type of table
dancing and whatnot that it is today."

Frank never testified before the McClellan Committee, but
reportedly had a phone chat with Bobby Kennedy in early
1959, though there is no record of it in the committee's papers.
He had more pressing problems locally. The Seattle City Council
was weighing whether to take away the Colacurcio brothers'
jukebox licenses, just as it took away their pinball license. Police
recommended the jukebox revocation based on Frank's strong-
arm tactics.

The council decided five to four to put the company on probation for the time being and to see what happened. Frank followed that up with a sort of thank-you letter, telling the council
that the false accusations about his criminal history, including
the accusations from the McClellan hearings, had damaged his
reputation. In a four-page letter, Colacurcio's longtime attorney, Joe Moschetto, said tales of Frank's influence peddling and
pinball syndication operation were "inaccurate and damaging

misrepresentations." After all, the claim that Frank was a racketeer had never been proved.

Frank asked for a hearing to clear his name. The council merely filed away the letter. The impression was left to linger. It clearly stressed him out. At age forty-two, Frank suffered a mild heart attack and was laid up for weeks.

By 1960, brother Bill, after his pinball license had been given to a competitor, went to court to get it back. Within a week, a pinball war broke out in Seattle. Several cars belonging to gambling figures were firebombed, along with the vehicle of mayoral candidate Gordon Newell, who'd taken a campaign stand against the games. The industry group, Amusement Association of Seattle, offered a $6,000 reward for the arrest and conviction of the pinball bombers (there had also been several related car bombings in 1958). The association's secretary-treasurer, Fred Galeno—who co-owned a racehorse with Teamster leader Frank Brewster—said his members would agree to take polygraph tests and sign affidavits to prove they told all they knew about the bombings. Police later took him and his members up on the offer, with Galeno first in line. He passed. Then Mayor Gordon Clinton said he would shut down pinball operations citywide if the bombings weren't solved. Deputy Police Chief (later head chief) Frank Ramon said his department had investigated five car bombings, three of them in recent months, but none were ever solved.

A former Colacurcio employee says some bombings were undertaken by his former bosses. "I don't know about the cars," who exactly bombed them, he says today, "but we used dynamite caps on the [rivals' amusement] machines. It was easy. You light the fuse and then just slap the cap onto the underside of the machine and walk out. Boom, coins all over, and you're down the street."

State officials pushed for new gambling laws and Seattle followed suit, no longer allowing pinball machines to pay off—indeed, for amusement only—and disallowing prizes for punchboard winners as well. A few days after the vote, squads of cops fanned out across the city to see if all businesses were complying. They collected exactly nine dice cups that businessmen had neglected to put away. Almost three hundred pinballs remained licensed as amusement devices, and more than sixty punchboard operations were approved for noncash rewards. But they didn't attract many customers since the county, unlike the city, continued to license pinball gambling.

Frank, though, had already moved into another field, something where clothing was optional. "From the vending business," he'd recall years later, "we loaned money to different bars, restaurants, lounges. And [when] they weren't able to pay, we took over several of them to make them [profitable]." One of his first joints was the Firelite Room—now a retro club called the Nitelite—in the Moore Hotel on Second Avenue, where, according to Frank, go-go dancing in Seattle first evolved into topless dancing fifty years ago. "I had a fellow from the Mideast that worked for me, and I seen the belly dancers and what they were doing and whatnot," he recalled. "That's how it became this type of table dancing and whatnot that it is today."

At forty-five Frank opened the Diamond Horseshoe, a beer garden and eatery at the 1962 Seattle World's Fair. He also quickly set a trend for his future in the bar and restaurant field by immediately getting busted: he'd hired teenage girls to go-go dance for him. Prosecutors said he advised the four minors to lie about their ages to state liquor inspectors. Colacurcio was booked and released on bond, and a justice court (today called municipal court) case dragged on for months before he was fined $500 and given a suspended six-month sentence for contributing to the delinquency of minors.

That didn't do much for Frank's image or, for that matter, for Mike Budnick, who was running for sheriff at the time with Frank's backing. Frank and brother Sam "played a part" in getting Budnick to run, the candidate admitted, but he wasn't getting much in return from the duo, other than $500 Sam donated. He used some of the money to hold a political fundraiser at Seattle's historic ballpark, Sick's Seattle Stadium, in the Rainier Valley. Unfortunately, the gate wasn't enough to cover costs of the big names he'd brought in to entertain folks, including showman George Jessel and jazz singer Anita O'Day (the extravaganza was promoted by George McFarland, best known as Spanky, the formerly chubby and angelic member of the *Our Gang* comedy movie series). "I mortgaged my home to help raise campaign funds, and I have nothing in my personal bank account," Budnick said, insisting he wasn't beholden to the Colacurcios. "No outsiders are going to get to Budnick!" he said.

By then, Frank was taking particular offense at slights to his character. In the wake of those late fifties McClellan hearings that fingered him as a racketeer, forty-year-old Frank met a teenager named Jacqueline Austin, a local hairdresser who was twenty-three years his junior. They were married on January 24, 1961, in Coeur d'Alene, Idaho. Known as Jackie, she would stay out of the headlines through most of their thirty-three years of marriage. In 1962 she gave birth to their son, Frank Francis Jr., and five years later the duo would buy the Sheridan Beach home, paying it off within a decade. With a wife and child, Frank now had a family to protect from his growing reputation.

His brother Bill was also feeling the heat and finally sold off the assets of the licenseless family pinball business for

$175,000. He claimed to be concentrating mostly on real estate deals, but was still sore about how the council took away his license. "Maybe this is the wrong town for me," he lamented. He was on to something. In early 1963, at age forty, he opened the door to federal agents standing on his doorstep with a summons. He was commanded to appear before a federal grand jury convened by then U.S. prosecutor Brock Adams—who'd go on to become a congressman, secretary of transportation under Jimmy Carter, and a one-term U.S. senator. Then eight women accused him of sexual misconduct ranging from sexual harassment to rape. He denied the claims but, facing certain defeat, chose to retire in 1993.

The grand jury launched a headline-making review of the pinball industry, which would later spill over into an even wider investigation of tolerance policy kickbacks and payoffs in the next decade. The jury probe was already in full swing when Bill was called to the stand in May 1963. A dozen defendants, in violation of the newest state law prohibiting cash payments from pinball machines, had already been charged with unlawful interstate transportation of gambling equipment: the machines. Under questioning, Bill twice refused to discuss a mysterious tape recording that FBI agents had seized from his Capitol Hill home six months earlier. Prosecutor Adams indicated the tape contained conversations between several pinball industry figures. Bill said he knew what was on the tape, "but I can't talk about it."

Faced with criminal contempt for balking before the grand jury, Bill claimed his testimony wasn't really needed, and at a hearing his attorney dramatically called prosecutor Adams to the witness stand and grilled him about the tape. Adams gave few details—the tape contained a general discussion of pinball operations, he said. A deputy prosecutor then objected, saying that forcing Adams to give specifics would violate the secrecy rule of grand jury testimony. U.S. Judge William Lindberg therein halted the inquiry. Bill agreed to talk to the grand jury the following month, but at the last minute balked one more time. Lindberg immediately dispatched him to prison for eight months. After three hours in custody, Bill cried uncle. He answered all thirteen questions that Adams asked about the tape.

Afterward, Bill told Don Duncan of the *Seattle Times* that he was tired of the Colacurcio family "being known as gangsters" and hoped his cooperation with prosecutors "will help clear the name." He was also worried the publicity was having a poor effect on his ailing mother, he said. "It wasn't fear of jail or anything like that. I called my mother from jail and she was crying, and I was afraid she might have another heart attack. She doesn't understand about contempt. To her, it's the same as murder." As Duncan wrote:

> "I told my mom that I've done nothing, that I've got immunity. I said that all the federals want me to do is to testify. But she doesn't understand."
>
> Colacurcio said he had been out of the pinball business about five years.
>
> "When I was in it, it was a business licensed by the City Council," he said.
>
> While Colacurcio spoke, he petted his German Shepherd, Tequito.
>
> "Tequito really charged when the police arrived to search my place," Colacurcio said with a smile. "When they opened the door, he tore right into them and out into the street.
>
> "I wish I'd never heard of the tape. I've got a feeling that they are trying to weave the whole case around me, that I'm the central figure. They told me they want me to testify again in September. Yes, I'll be around. I'm not going anywhere.

"It seems anything that happens in this town, we [Colacurcios] get blamed. I've got six brothers [five, unless he was errantly including himself] and three sisters. My sisters get digs all the time, like 'Oh, your brothers are gangsters.' How would you like that?"

Colacurcio telephoned his mother at her Bow Lake home this morning. She was pleased he was home again.

What was on the tape? Bill Colacurcio clammed up, and authorities didn't want to talk about it. The defendants charged with pinball violations all agreed to plead no contest and were fined. The tape was never played in court and is forever sealed in a court repository.

But, says a former Colacurcio associate today, the tape included specific details of the payoff system by businesses to keep police from busting pinball and other vice operators, including how the money worked its way up the line to City Hall.

"The tape was a recording Bill made [apparently surreptitiously] of a city councilman describing how the payoff system worked, how the cops picked up the money and then passed it down the line—to him and others," says the associate, who ran bars and hotels for Colacurcio. "I understand that they played the tape for him [the council member, whose name the associate couldn't remember] one day and he suddenly felt too old to seek re-election."

EROGENOUS ZONES

Pike's Peak

"After the last dirty film ended at six-thirty this morning, I went
down and woke up the last three customers."

In 1964 Seattle mayor J. D. "Dorm" Braman revived the city
tolerance policy, assuming it ever really died. He'd been sup-
ported by high-rolling operators of gaming clubs and took up
their cause in office, restating the notion that vice was easier to
police if it was licensed and regulated. It was also around that time
that Frank was expanding his area of sinful expertise, becoming a
full-time restaurateur: a "Nightlife figure" as the libel-conscious
newspapers called him. He had opened the Magic Inn on Union
Street and the Firelite Room on Second Avenue, where, by 1965,
he featured go-go dancing on a regular basis. That helped turn
downtown Seattle and its uphill neighborhoods into a carnival
of life. It was, jazz historian Paul de Barros writes, "a time when
Seattle, which now rolls up its streets at ten o'clock, was full of
people walking up and down the sidewalk after midnight. When
you could buy a newspaper at the corner of 14th and Yesler
from a man called Neversleep—at three in the morning. When

limousines pulled up to the 908 Club all night, disgorging celebrities and wealthy women wearing diamonds and furs."

Pike Street had somewhat lower expectations. It was Seattle's zipper, running east from the waterfront crotch, awash with card rooms and bars, con men and streetwalkers, porn houses and topless joints. Much of Pike's denizens assembled in such places as Pizza Nick's, a hole-in-the-wall known as the Abruzzi Pizza House. That's where Nick stood in the window and tossed dough for thirty-eight years. It was located where Niketown now stands. As Nick said after being told his building would be coming down in 1994: "There's some kinda tennis shoe store goin' in here." To its last day, Nick's still had its original air conditioner, refrigeration, and, for the most part, its so-called decor: fake brick walls and Nick, the real deal. At the tables had sat a legendary mix of prostitutes and pols, prizefighters and priests, cops and comedians. But the main attraction was Nick, in a white apron, extending a white-floured hand and saying things like, "If these walls could talk, it would be a miracle!"

Across from Nick's was a bowling alley above a cigar store called the Carcinogen. The alley and store were both run by a businessman and sometime porn dealer named Slim Montgomery, who would be arrested several times by telephone. The cops had gone through the magazines on his racks—from *Knob Job* to *Juicy Juggs*—and knew porn when they felt it. They returned to headquarters, got approval for a bust, but didn't feel like driving back to the store to pick up Slim. He had seemed like a nice guy, so they called on the phone. Slim answered and said, "OK, I'll come down." That happened a few times, meaning an expensive cab ride now and then, but Slim said he eventually wised up. "I bought a bus pass."

Around the corner was the Nikko Garden, a seventies go-go joint where, if you complained, a barmaid swatted you with a stick. The nearby Caballero was a topless joint where a blind man was once seen sitting in the front row, tapping his cane to the musical beat. Across the street was the Gay Nineties, which actually was gay in the seventies. The Club Chi Chi, all crappy and wonderful, was up Pike near the Flick, the street's last porn theater. The day the Flick closed, its sole employee called the *Seattle Times*: "After the last dirty film ended at six-thirty this morning," he said, "I went down and woke up the last three customers. The workmen are starting to take out anything of value right now. They should be done in a coupla minutes."

Nearby, on Union Street, was Bob's Chili Parlor, later replaced by the Sheraton Hotel. Old-timers recalled the night that parlor owner Bob Kevo slugged a man named Russian Nick, knocking him over a table in the upstairs card room. Russian Nick had been impatient for a seat at a dice game, and Kevo was an equally impatient maître d'. Nick took out a gun and shot Kevo in the brain. In court, claiming self-defense, he walked. Kevo had attacked him first.

At the bottom of Pike, where it hits First Avenue, was the old Turf eatery and bar, having relocated after losing its longtime space on Third Avenue. Pensioners liked the inexpensive menu, hookers came in to rest their feet, hustlers traded watches for drinks, and the bouncer was once a candidate for Washington secretary of state. Democrat "Big John" McKee, who in 1984 drew the ballots of 667,985 people in a losing effort against incumbent Republican Ralph Munro, was ejecting from the bar some of the same people who said they voted for him.

It seemed a mostly mellow joint, but bartender Jerry Gene noted, "Sometimes it's like the United Nations with knives." He counted his wounds. "Let's see, I've been punched, stabbed, broke my leg chasing a guy—but I also saved a life giving mouth-to-mouth. I always try to help the people who don't hit me." At the end of the night, Gene put on his coat and picked up a dollar tip. "I'll be here tomorrow," he said. "I need the agony."

Across from the Turf was the Mirror Tavern, the kind of place you'd get thrown *into*. The Turf eventually relocated up the street again, but the Mirror joined the pantheon of dive bars and porn joints drowned by the progress of the nineties and thereafter. So did the Liberty Jewelry & Loan pawnshop whose owner, Martin Levy, and his daughter and son-in-law all went to prison in 2008 for selling stolen goods bought from drug addicts. In its place today is the Hard Rock Cafe, with its rooftop bar. Next door, on the First and Pike corner, is a Starbucks, fashionably renovated in 2009. They are part of a new world where bartenders will likely never again have the experience of old-time barkeep Uncle Tommy, who used to hold forth on nearby Pine Street in Ciro's Rickshaw Room—owned by two of Frank Colacurcio's sisters.

"I turn around, and a naked guy is sitting at my bar at six in the morning," Tommy said a few years back. "'OK,' I think, 'heeere we go.'" As he recalled the conversation:

Tommy: What can I do for you?

Naked Guy: Drink.

Tommy: Sorry, can't serve you.

Naked Guy: What! Just because I'm naked?

Tommy: No. Because I know you don't have any money on you.

Naked Guy got up and left. "And if he had money on him," Tommy added, "I still woulda refused. Who knows where he was keeping it?"

Lusty Ladies and Gentlemen

Happy True would "buy pints because they were flat. Fifths in round bottles would have saved him a heck of a slug in money. But they were uncomfortable to sleep on."

The intersection where Pike Street runs into First Avenue is known to some wildlife sociologists as the Crossroads of Mental Health. For decades, street crazies and druggies occupied the four corners, along with prostitutes, players, and partyers. A pint-size Scotsman named Andy Brodie, who went by the street name of "Half-Horse Half-Alligator"—it had something to do with the size of his "groinal area" he said—once aptly described the First and Pike scene: he saw a buddy in the crowd crossing the intersection, and when he shouted "Hey, asshole!" *everyone* in the street turned around.

Besides bars and hockshops, there were peep shows and amusement arcades lining First Avenue's blocks from the fifties into the eighties. The arcades, recalled likeable Seattle police lieutenant Frank Ottersbach, who walked the avenue beat in the fifties and sixties, featured dirty movies in coin-operated panorama viewers. "We were instructed to raid them from time to

Seattle police raid an illegal peep show in 1954. (Photo: *Seattle Post-Intelligencer* Collection, MOHAI)

time," he said, and the Seattle Police Department (SPD) supplied him and others with dimes to go watch the shows and then bust the operators. The first time he watched one of the movies, Ottersbach said, "There were two girls sitting on chairs. One had underwear on—panties and a bra. The other had a housecoat on, and once in a while she let the thing flop open. You couldn't see the whole thing—none of the garbage you see today."

Joe Wenzl, a Seattle longshoreman in those days, recalled how he and others would work hard on the waterfront and play hard on the Avenue, where bartenders doubled as financial consultants. "If they were broke they'd go in and hit the bartender up for whatever their word was good for. This was our bank, our social club," Wenzl said. "Evidently, now everybody belongs to a tennis club. I don't think they can borrow money there."

David Edenso, who lived in the LaSalle Apartments—Nellie Curtis's onetime Pike Place Market whorehouse—said the neighborhood was filled with characters attracted by downtown's vices. An old seaman named Happy True, for example, lived in a sleeping room with a two-burner hot plate and passed out on his mattress of whiskey. "He'd buy up two, three cases of pints of whiskey and line them up under his mattress," said Edenso. "He'd buy pints because they were flat. Fifths in round bottles would have saved him a heck of a slug in money. But they were uncomfortable to sleep on."

Included in that roster of characters was tattoo artist Danny Danzel, who learned his ink art by tattooing dogs when he was a kid. His longtime First Avenue Tattoo Shop offered up "automatic tattoo removal": a tank of live piranhas. He practiced his art ethically—when a man asked to have a tattoo put on his face, Danny told the customer he'd likely come to regret it. So instead he drew the tattoo on with a pencil, and the man never came back. The mean streets were made a little sweeter by Backwards Louie, who walked everywhere backward. He liked to borrow money for a few drinks, but when people saw him coming, they crossed the street. So he devised an act. He always appeared to be walking away when in fact he was walking backward—pumping his knees smartly up and down like a drill team. Once a victim closed in, he'd suddenly spin about and put his hand out.

"I hate to ask," Louie was once heard to say, "but a dollar would get me through college."

"What college is that?"

"A cheap one."

Other performers of downtown's faded street show included a seventies couple, George and Pansy, Seattle's only mother-son funeral-attending team. In tandem, they also regularly attended weddings, baby christenings, and private parties, usually uninvited and often taking photos with filmless cameras. After Pansy died, little George carried on the ritual of sitting atop Pansy's grave on her birthday, having a picnic and watching baseball on a portable TV. They had lived in a music-filled home up on Capitol Hill, packed with twelve pianos.

The late King Olaf, meanwhile, left a vice record no one will ever break: most arrests, drunk in public, single person. In the twenty-five years records were kept, until the drunk-in-public law was repealed in the seventies, Olaf was arrested 401 times and sentenced to 10,680 days in jail—he served 7,711 of them. That comes to more than twenty years locked up. Olaf had the right attitude. "Say what you want," he said. "I always had a place to stay."

Once, according to a police report, an American Indian with a rope lassoed a passing First Avenue cab in Pioneer Square. It was culturally significant enough to make the *New York Times*.

In the seventies, there were fourteen downtown porno theaters/dirty book stores, such as the Champ Arcade and Green Parrot. There were also nine hockshops, including Myer's Music and pawn store, where, in the fifties, Al Hendrix bought teenage son Jimi his first guitar. And squeezed in among the greasy spoons and flophouses were twenty-five taverns. Not restaurant bars, like those on upscale First Avenue today, but real taverns: the Alaska, Boulder, Oxford, Shellback, and Beaver among them. There were so many that the game was to have one beer at each pub—traveling up one side of the street from Pioneer Square to the Pike Place Market, then down the other—without passing out. A huge fellow named Tiny Freeman, who ran for the U.S. Senate from his office at the J & M Café bar, claims to have made it all the way up one side and partway down the other before losing his lunch on Union Street. In later years, he was shocked to see how many places had lost out to progress and disappeared. "The tradition of the Skid Road bar—in a town where Skid Road was invented—is in a sad state," he said. "It's really hard to find a place that people won't go into anymore." Among the joints on the endurance course was the York Lunch near First and Pike, where, fifty years after women were given the right to vote, owners were still refusing to serve females at the bar. It just wasn't dignified for ladies to sit there, a bartender said; besides, they usually got drunk and nasty. The owners eased the policy after a couple of women set off a small bomb one morning on the York's doorstep.

Some of First Avenue's traditions lived on at the Lusty Lady, the fully nude dance club down the street from Pike Place Market and across from the Seattle Art Museum. The nudie joint and the highfalutin museum lived in harmony, even when the Lady's marquee celebrated civic events, such as Seafair ("Chicks Ahoy!"), the World Trade Organization riots ("Nude

World Order"), or holidays ("Happy Spanksgiving!"). Dancers performed fully nude on a stage surrounded by paying customers in a series of individual booths. They peered at the stage through windows featuring electric shades, which rose and fell depending on how much time a customer purchased by putting quarters in a coin box. Other booths featured dirty movies: high-tech panoramas. It was a business long managed by women, where thousands of quarters flowed through the coin boxes daily—a million dollar annual operation in Seattle and at a companion club in San Francisco. Strippers entertained customers they liked and those they were wary about. All were made bearable by the glass that separated them from the dancers. While they could see their "clients" masturbating, the dancers were often thinking of mundane chores they had to do after work, such as pick up milk and baby food. Most had a good sense of humor about performing nude. "You should have seen the last guy I had," said a dancer who worked in a "private pleasures" booth. He opened his coat and he was wearing a slip, which he pulled up, exposing himself. "He's nude from the waist down, wanking away while I dance for him, and in the middle of it he says, 'How do you like my legs?' I burst out laughing. Kind of ruined his mood."

Many of the dancers were single moms or college students and had also worked at Frank Colacurcio's strip joints. "There were grad students; there were law students working when I was there," recalled Elisabeth Eaves, who went on to become an author and an editor at *Forbes* magazine. "There were a couple of real estate agents; there definitely were some moms. A trapeze artist, I think she's still there. Some artists and writers. It was a pretty cool bunch of women." They were typically poor, did it for the money, and weren't particularly interested in the sex. Some had boyfriends, and almost all had followers, if not stalkers, who tried to see them outside the club. "Under no circumstances ever do that!" one said in an interview. "There may be a few nice guys. But they all turn out to be creeps." The girls also got good advice from one of the Lady's managers, June, who protected and educated them. Among the lessons: Don't do pornography, no matter how desperate you are. "The live show ends with your shift," June would say. "Video is forever."

Thankfully, this little bit of history continued to spice up fading First Avenue even after the lowbrow Lady got caught up in the high-stakes game of downtown real estate development a few years ago. The Lady's tacky, narrow little building at 1315 First Avenue appeared doomed when a group of heavyweight developers, including a billionaire, a wealthy venture capitalist, and a former Seattle mayor, aimed their wrecking ball at Peaches, Kitten, and Trixie. They and their nudie house, it appeared, were about to become the next victims of the condofornication of Seattle.

Then the inconceivable happened: in a city where rapacious new development effortlessly bulldozes fading history, someone said no to money. Christto Tolias and his family, longtime owners of the century-old, mostly vacant structure housing the peep-show theater, refused to sell the property. The family rejected an offer of "several" millions of dollars from ex-mayor Paul Schell and his fellow hotel/condo developers, including cellular magnate Bruce McCaw and investment whiz Tom Alberg. Attorney John Sinsheimer said the family's motives to not sell were personal and financial. "They like the building. It's a good investment with a steady income stream," he said, "and they just wanted to keep it." Property records list the building's birth date as 1900 and the site's assessed value at $2 million. In earlier days, the building was a seaman's bar and hotel called the Seven

Seas. It became one of the city's first gay nudie theaters, the Sultan, before the Lusty Lady moved in around 1985.

After the rejection, Schell and partners in the new twenty-one-story, $120 million Four Seasons hotel and condo tower at First Avenue and Union Street had to regroup. With no other option, they made the Toliases another offer: they would buy air rights above the Lusty building. While the old joint would remain, the agreement would allow the developers to extend such aerial structures as decks and balconies overhead. The Toliases accepted. Marvelous. The big developers not only didn't get their prized property, they paid $850,000 for thin air.

The strippers, among the last practitioners in Seattle's once-thriving old vice district, stayed on as the neighbors who walked around in the nude. But while the club could outlast detractors and developers, it couldn't weather the economy. In 2010 the Lady's owners announced the strip joint was going tits up, closing its doors. Comptroller and co-owner Darrell Davis said income had dropped 60 percent in the past decade. Alas, Seattleites didn't want to pay to see naked ladies anymore. They could get that for free at home—on their computers.

Déjà Vu All Over

"I'd much rather have been allowed to open a nudie club years ago than have to go to court. I'd have made a lot more money."

Low-life preservationists who rue upscaling could only lament, as did late architect and politically incorrect civic preservationist Victor Steinbrueck, that "the first victim of 'progress' is always raunchiness." He was referring not only to the old joints on First Avenue and Pike Street, but to the oases of vice that surrounded them—the erstwhile dirty movie houses of Seattle, for example, many owned by onetime porn king Roger Forbes. Himself a cultural eyesore to his critics, Forbes now controls the nationwide Déjà Vu nude dance chain. He was a rival to Frank Colacurcio, with three nude clubs downtown, including the Déjà Vu near First and Pike, and a club that competed with Frank's nude club, Rick's, in Seattle's Lake City neighborhood.

Forbes is also a multimillionaire, though his clubs tend not to bring in the money Frank's operations did. Investigators say that's because there's typically no sex trade between customers and dancers at his clubs. Though Déjà Vu clubs, such as the one in Federal Way, have been busted in the past, undercover

officers in recent years repeatedly tried to solicit sex from Seattle
Déjà Vu dancers, they say, but got no takers (actually, some of
the girls at Forbes's Lake City club directed them to Rick's, saying they were more likely to get lucky there). Not surprisingly,
Rick's outdrew the Déjà Vu five-to-one in customer count. The
Vu also had no secluded VIP area or condom machine, as Rick's
did. Washington State Department of Revenue records reflect
the end result: during 2006 and 2007, Rick's reported $10.3
million in gross revenue, while Déjà Vu took in $3.2 million.
"We run a dance club," Forbes said in a 2009 interview. "They
[the Colacurcio clan] run whatever in the hell it is they run."

Forbes originally made his money by altering Seattle's
sex-biz landscape with a lucrative little chain of porn theaters,
beginning in downtown Seattle. With a $15,000 loan from
friends and family in 1971, at age twenty-eight, he began a
two-decade-long career operating a string of Northwest porno
houses. Among them was the Midtown on First and the Winter
Garden on Third. Due in part to his Playtime Theaters chain,
Seattle in the seventies was home to eleven porn flicks. Fearful
for their children and weary of looking at the long lines for *Deep
Throat*, church and civic leaders conspired to run Forbes out
of town, only to constantly collide with the First Amendment.
They shifted their strategy to rezoning him out of town, and
that was more successful, starting with a legal case filed by the
suburban city of Renton.

Forbes challenged that legal blockade all the way to the U.S.
Supreme Court. Unfortunately, in doing so, he also forever
altered the way vice would be regulated here and across America:
the court ruled that a Renton city zoning ordinance banning
porn theaters from school, church, and residential neighborhoods was constitutional. The 1986 ruling in *City of Renton
v. Playtime Theaters Inc.*, authored by Chief Justice William

Rehnquist, found that "the ordinance is a valid governmental response to the serious problems created by adult theaters and satisfies the dictates of the First Amendment." Renton's law therein became the law of the land.

Its effects would also reverberate constantly through Frank's world, such as when he challenged a Tacoma-area ordinance in 1998. In *DCR Inc. v. Pierce County*—DCR was one of Frank's businesses, which owned Fox's nudie club in the Tacoma area—the Washington Supreme Court cited the Renton case in upholding a county-imposed ten-foot rule, forcing dancers to keep their distance from customers. Frank and son Frankie vainly argued it was a First Amendment violation.

The high court's ruling didn't affect Forbes's string of Seattle, Tacoma, and Eastside theaters as much as the video revolution later would. He stayed ahead of the wave by steering his investments into nude dancing with the chain that has used the slogan "fifty beautiful women and three ugly ones." For the most part, the porn king chose to relinquish his old turf, including downtown's last porn theater, the Midtown, which was remodeled and reborn in 1999 as an upscale salon. To the added satisfaction of City Hall, the developer who bought the theater from Forbes was also the wife of Seattle's then–city attorney Mark Sidran.

However, Forbes went on to get even, creating quite the ironic spectacle along the way. In 2009 it was a howl to see attorneys for the city and for Forbes sitting side by side in court, facing off against attorneys for the Seattle Mariners. The uncomfortable scenario in King County Superior Court was the result of an attempt by Forbes to open yet another downtown nudie joint, this one near Safeco Field, home of Ichiro, Griffey, and the Mariners. After staving off Forbes and others through a moratorium against any new strip clubs downtown, City Hall suddenly found itself in the awkward spot of defending them. A federal court in 2005 found the moratorium unconstitutional, thanks to a lawsuit by another club operator, Bob Davis, who'd been refused a permit. The city officially lifted the moratorium in 2007, enabling Forbes, whose First and Pike Déjà Vu was grandfathered in, to open a new club, Little Darlings, off Westlake Avenue, and plan a third joint, DreamGirls, on First Avenue South, a few doors down from Edgar Martinez Drive. As the foul tip flies, that's about four hundred feet from Safeco Field's main entry.

The Mariners objected. They maintained that a strip club that close wouldn't comply with a provision in the Land Use Code that prohibits strip joints within eight hundred feet of public parks and open spaces. Safeco was a park, they contended. (A ballpark, so to speak, but then so was Forbes's club, so to speak.) Furthermore, said the M's, a nudie joint would harm children and the national pastime. In a court brief, Mariners attorney Melody McCutcheon noted that approximately 26 million people attended M's games from 1999 through 2007, at least 3.6 million of whom were children. "The Mariners have a significant interest in maintaining a family-friendly atmosphere at Safeco Field and its associated public open space areas," she stated. "A strip club in such close proximity . . . will impair enjoyment of those facilities and will discourage families with children from attending events there."

In a sense, it was a case of good vs. evil. But which was which? Safeco's fans drank beer and ogled Junior and Ichiro. Strip club fans drank soda pop and ogled Peaches and Candy. Which was the greater threat to democracy?

Not Roger, the court ruled in 2009. The city permit to allow the club was properly granted, a judge concluded. The M's appealed, but months later struck an agreement with Forbes: it wouldn't further contest his permit if he agreed to tone down his signage—no garish "Live Girls" neon, for example, and no outdoor-video pictures of women when Safeco events are aimed at children. The club also would not be allowed to use barkers or amplified sound to attract customers. Deal, said Forbes. DreamGirls opened to rave reviews from baseball fans in 2010.

Bob Davis, the man whose lawsuit paved the way for Forbes, didn't fare as well. Though he had made more than $850,000 in two lawsuits of his own, suing and then settling with the cities of Seattle and Bothell for illegally thwarting his own club permit applications, he, as of this writing, has yet to open a club of his own. Among other ventures, he'd planned to turn a North Seattle pancake house, called Cyndy's, into a nudie joint. But he ran into neighborhood opponents who complained it would be too close to a school, a zoning violation. Davis also said his girlfriend, who disliked his nudie effort, bailed on him, and that while he made a bundle on his court challenges, he never really got rich. "Most of it has gone to my legal fees," he said. He just wished he'd been as financially and legally prosperous as his idol Forbes, or at least like Frank Colacurcio. "I'd much rather have been allowed to open a nudie club years ago than have to go to court," he said. "I'd have made a lot more money."

He lamented the old days, when Seattle had tolerance for this sort of thing.

SEATTLE
EXPOSED

Vice, Film at 11

Frank's business, "if not illegal, verges on the immoral."

Following Dorm Braman's 1964 tolerance revival, how was the new policy working? Much like the old one, Seattle began to learn in 1967 from a series in the *Seattle Times* by John Wilson and Marshall Wilson. Known as the Wilson twins, though not related, they spoke with Skid Road and First Avenue tavern operators who claimed they were being forced to make payoffs to police. The Wilsons kept low to the ground, spying on the cops as they made cash pickups, although the cops spied them as well: sitting in their car on a stakeout one night, John's coat sleeve caught on a steering wheel ring and set off the car horn, causing a couple of cops to notice and quickly move away. The twins nonetheless determined that payoffs were widespread. Their series also revealed how on-duty officers whiled away the hours in one tavern, gambling after hours. (Unreported then, but years later confirmed by a bar operator, police also used to take over a Pioneer Square eatery called Swannie's for after-hours target practice, using live rounds to shoot beer bottles and other objects set atop a high ledge on the back bar.) As the Wilsons would write in a follow-up story, however, "Official reaction was more of indignation than of concern."

Police Chief Frank Ramon expressed shock at the series, but played it down as misconduct among a few officers. Mayor Braman, a onetime lumber and hardware dealer, said he was interested in "building a better city" and less interested in running the police department. He formed a committee to investigate, but gave it no powers. After studying the issue, the committee found nothing to justify criminal charges.

The *P-I* also came up with a rollicking exposé later that year, a long series of stories by ace reporter Orman Vertrees, revealing that an unnamed suspect in a 1957 jukebox bombing was still in the jukebox business ten years later. The series also fed off the McClellan Committee hearings, noting that Joe McLaughlin was still a pinball licensee even though he had been named in the rackets hearing as a vice and gambling organizer. Vertrees noted that public officials claimed the tolerance system keeps out "Chicago gangsters" and other mobs, while critics wondered if it truly was just a guise to allow local gangsters to lock up control of the multimillion-dollar vice industry. His story cited previously unreleased documents from the rackets committee that concluded the Seattle coin machine trade group was formed to restrain trade and fix prices.

The weeklong series in November 1967, along with follow-up stories, documented payoffs and tax cheating in the pinball industry; it also coughed up some new details about Seattle's favorite suspected racketeer, Frank Colacurcio, who was quietly building what looked like a regional empire of vice. He'd bought into five historic Washington hotels in Centralia, Wenatchee, Mount Vernon, Port Angeles, and Aberdeen, where his brother Patrick was in charge at the Morck Hotel, thought to have become a haven for prostitution in the post–Nellie Curtis era.

Police said prostitutes were operating out of some of the other hotels, as well as at Frank's Firelite Room at the Moore Hotel in Seattle.

A Colacurcio associate named Art Baldwin, who'd earlier been arrested in Seattle for possession of illegal gambling devices, had taken over operations at the Lee Hotel in Port Angeles. He turned the hotel's Cavalier Room into a hangout for "scantily clad women," as horrified civic officials referred to them. A Port Angeles City Council member complained it wasn't right of Baldwin "to use sex to sell liquor," while Mayor Charlie Willson wrote the state Liquor Control Board to complain. Colacurcio's operation, "if not illegal," Willson said, "verges on the immoral." Of course, as Frank had said before of his vice clubs, he was just giving the public what it wanted. And apparently what Port Angeles's male population wanted. Said Port Angeles Police Department Lieutenant Roy Morgan: "There were an awful lot of wives around town that if you said you were going to the Lee, the hair was in the beans." They were, in other words, mad.

Still loosely connected to Frank's operations, Art Baldwin would later go on to run topless clubs in Nashville and Oklahoma City, amassing criminal indictments for tax evasion, cocaine possession, and bribery. As part of one plea deal, he cooperated with the FBI in 1978 in an investigation of payoffs and bribes to public officials in Tennessee, which ultimately led to the arrest of three aides to former governor Ray Blanton. Baldwin eventually did a ten-year prison term for the attempted fire bombings of rival clubs. In a 2003 book, *An Act of State: The Execution of Martin Luther King*, Baldwin was reported to have offered a fellow inmate a contract in the late seventies to kill another Tennessee inmate, James Earl Ray, the assassin of Martin Luther King Jr. The conspiracy theory was that Baldwin, as a government informant, was acting on behalf of the feds who wanted Ray dead—in an attempt to contain the truth about who really killed Dr. King. The Department of Justice looked into the alleged Baldwin contract offer but found nothing to support it. Freed in the eighties, Baldwin said he found God in prison and went straight thereafter. Even though he was often out of work, he told the Memphis *Commercial Appeal* in 1993, "I would not trade this Art Baldwin [for] the million-dollar Art Baldwin. All the time I had clubs and had all that money I was miserable." He died in 1997 at age fifty-nine.

One scantily clad woman from the Lee Hotel, Vertrees reported, also showed up at the Firelite Room, where, police said, she was arrested for propositioning an undercover cop. That suggested the girls were traveling hotel to hotel on a sex circuit. Vertrees reported the Firelite's cabaret license was held in the name of one of Frank's sisters, Frances. Down the street at Seattle's Savoy Hotel, the license for another operation secretly run by Frank, Nero's Room, was in the name of another sister, Jessie. It operated under the business name of B. J. Enterprises. It, too, was known for its scantily clads: a year earlier, cops broke up what they called a prostitution ring operating out of the hotel.

The extended family was hard at work elsewhere as well, the *P-I* discovered. Frank's brother Bill tried to buy into a Las Vegas club, Pussy Cat A Go-Go, a year earlier, seeking a 49 percent interest for $100,000. That failed even though he had $700,000 in a Seattle bank. He and brother Sam were still listed as top officials of Colacurcio Bros. Amusement Co., which at that point was still the second-largest Seattle jukebox company, with 103 licensed locations. Another jukebox operator who was married to Colacurcio sister, Rosie, had been allowed to obtain music licenses even though police said he, too, was just running a dummy corporation for the Colacurcios.

The *P-I* zeroed in on how those innocent bingo games around Seattle were turning big profits for their operators, some of them tied in with Frank. Pensioners were also being victimized by bingo games that were supposedly run as charities, but were earning some operators up to $320,000 a year, the paper said. The biggest offender seemed to be a man named Charles Berger, who did time at McNeil Island (then federal) penitentiary for tax evasion and ran the Lifeline Club off First Avenue, in a large second-floor room in the Pike Place Market. Berger's club was up the street from another parlor called ALFA (Assisting Legislation for Aging), run by a man named Harry Hoffman. His name seemed familiar, and it was: during the Tacoma crime hearings held by Al Rosellini in the fifties, he'd been linked to the payoff system there.

Both parlors featured bingo games at a dime a card, which were thrown away after each game. The gamesters were predominately housewives and the elderly, spending a few bucks or so on cards, but rarely at a profit. To illustrate the futility of trying to win at the clubs, a *P-I* undercover bingo player lost $395 while winning only $55 in a four-month spree. The paper also gave its agents money to go into card rooms, where they also lost badly—and discovered some card decks were being marked.

Though not well known, among the *P-I*'s losing amateur agents was Orman Vertrees's brother-in-law, a young man named Mike Lowry. He played cards on the paper's tab and was quite poor at it. He went on to become a congressman and in 1992 was elected Washington's governor. "I went in and played cards in the back room of one of those places," Lowry said in 2010. "I wasn't even in their league. But then I think that was the plan. What good would the story have been if we all won?"

By 1968, both the *Times* and the *P-I* were steadily reporting on the widespread corruption, protection racket, and booming bookmaking industry, also linking longtime King County prosecutor Charles O. "Chuck" Carroll to gambling and determining pinballs alone were bringing in $5 million a year to the industry. *Seattle* magazine profiled Carroll as well, questioning his judicial tactics, depicting him as a vengeful prosecutor who held out harsh treatment for blacks, and calling for his resignation.

The *P-I* memorably provided photographic evidence, grainy as it was, to its readers, showing county pinball kingpin Ben Cichy allegedly delivering money to prosecutor Carroll's home. Cichy headed up Farwest Novelty Co., which held the master license to operate 1,540 county pinballs, pool tables, and bowling games in local taverns. Thanks to a legal opinion by Carroll that gaming was allowed despite some conflicting laws, a county tolerance policy quietly flourished outside Seattle, to Cichy's profit and delight. Reporter Vertrees, noting that Cichy and Carroll were "on opposite sides of the fence of life," wrote that the two had been having regular monthly meet-ups, watched over by the *P-I*. "What could possibly be the nature of such liaison between men of such diverse callings," Vertrees asked in print, "a prosecutor and a pillar of the pinball fellowships?"

Joel Connelly, now a *P-I* columnist in his sixties, says he well remembers that sneaky Cichy photo, taken by the paper's Dave Potts, who hung out on a nearby balcony night after night to snap the pic. "I saw it when I was young," Connelly says. "I was amazed at what it meant. That's when I knew I wanted to be a newspaperman."

State attorney general John J. O'Connell brought in Ralph Salerno, former supervisor of New York Police Department detectives, to consult with investigators, saying he knew of no other major U.S. city with a gambling-tolerant police approaching Seattle's. The editorialists and letter writers demanded an investigation. But as the pressure increased for a widespread probe into who was paying whom, Cichy, on May 30, 1969, conveniently drowned off the dock of his Eastside home at Yarrow Point. Foul play was suspected, yet never proved. He was an excellent swimmer found in five feet of water.

Mayor Braman had resigned a few months earlier to accept an appointment as a U.S. Department of Transportation assistant secretary in the Nixon administration and was replaced by interim mayor Floyd Miller, a Council member hoping to clean a little house. He handed limited power to three assistant police chiefs—Frank Moore, George Fuller, and A. C. "Tony" Gustin—to clean up the department. In that spirit, Gustin and Fuller backed what turned out to be a historic September 24, 1969, raid on the Lifeline Club bingo parlor without telling Chief Ramon in advance. When Ramon left town on a brief vacation, Gustin and his flying squad swooped into the Lifeline and cited about eighty players for gambling. The charges were later dropped, but, more importantly, Gustin got what he came for: evidence of illegal gambling and payoffs to politicians. In the records were names of Council members and deputy prosecutors; the wife of a former sheriff was also on the club's payroll. And so much for bingo as a benign vice: ledgers indicated the club was raking in up to $2 million a year.

Seattle's corrupt tolerance system suddenly went into spasms. Chief Ramon declared there would be no further such raids. The three assistant chiefs fired back, saying Ramon was interfering with their lawful duties. Led by the rebellious Gustin, they issued a game-breaking ultimatum: Ramon had to step down, or they would ask for reassignment, which would be an embarrassment for City Hall.

As that impasse smoldered, an investigative report by KOMO-TV's Don McGaffin revealed copies of checks proving that money from bingo clubs in the city and burbs had gone to the campaign funds of seventeen public officials, including city, county, and state legislators, along with Sheriff Jack Porter. McGaffin also laid out the story so far, detailing the Lifeline raid and Chief Ramon's apparent attempts to downplay it. The chief had also cut funding to his vice unit after the raids, slowing down enforcement efforts, and, it turned out, had released club operator Charlie Berger's gun from an evidence locker, as a favor to Berger. Ex-con Berger, McGaffin said, had a gun permit that had been issued by Sheriff Porter's office, and the gun had once belonged to a deputy sheriff whose wife worked at Berger's club. The full story began to shape up, and the crusading McGaffin made the point to viewers that this wasn't about some innocuous game of chance:

> One of the peculiar and sustaining myths of our time is that bingo is a game played by gray-haired little ladies in church basements for prizes such as electric blankets or toasters. This is the purest kind of nonsense. Practically every knowledgeable vice squad detective knows that bingo long ago turned into a huge commercial gambling operation.

At interim mayor Miller's urging, Ramon agreed to retire—or be fired—in October 1969, a month before the general election of a new mayor who would be sure to replace the chief; Wes Uhlman, who won the election, had said as much in his campaign. The palace revolt by his assistants had succeeded in ousting Ramon after a twenty-eight-year, often-praiseworthy career, tarnished in the end by scandal.

Frank Colacurcio, meanwhile, was dealing with the recent death of his father, William, who died at age seventy-eight, survived by his widow, Christina. That didn't seem to slow Frank's criminal career much: he was facing a new assault charge. A former employee said Frank beat him up outside the Firelite, in front of a cop who didn't step in to help. Frank was later arrested and released on bail. The man, Vernon Harvey, twenty-seven, was a former Firelite bartender who turned out to be a police informant. Frank was apparently reacting to that discovery when Harvey stopped in to pick up a letter of recommendation for his next job and got a beating instead.

During a three-day trial, Harvey claimed a cop had been nearby but never intervened. He said the cop told him, after he was kicked and punched by Frank on the sidewalk, to "just forget" the incident. "If I didn't back off and drop charges against Frank Colacurcio," he recalled the cop saying, "Frank would take care of me." The cop said Harvey must have misunderstood him, he was just indicating revenge was a waste of time. Another cop, a detective, sort of balanced the record, telling the court the department wasn't prone to do favors for Frank, who was being investigated for other assaults, as well as illegal narcotics and promoting prostitution at the Firelite, Ciro's, Magic Inn, and his central Washington club, the Corral in Yakima.

Frank didn't testify at the 1969 trial, but was rated as an outstanding individual by his sister Frances—referred to by her married name, Mrs. James Schmitz—who claimed under oath she owned and operated the Firelite. Frank was merely the assistant manager, she said. Frank's brother Pat, who worked at the Magic Inn, said his brother was quite the gentleman and wouldn't go around hitting people. Frank nonetheless was convicted of third-degree assault, a class C felony, and fined $500.

It was just another slightly irritating exercise for Frank. A more costly one was coming his way as, this time, he and the tolerance policy headed to court.

Tolerance on Trial

A cop told him that bar work can be dangerous, and "I'm sure
you don't want anything to happen to your little girl."

By the seventies, Seattle was destined to host dueling grand
juries—one federal, one state, both looking into the surfacing
story of Seattle vice. Frank was indicted by a federal grand jury for
racketeering, along with bingo parlor operators Charlie Berger
and Harry Hoffman. Hoffman was accused of making political
payoffs, and Berger was accused of paying Colacurcio $3,000 a
month per bingo location; in return, Frank would "guarantee"
that cops would maintain a tolerance policy and overlook gambling violations at the two men's parlors. U.S. Attorney Stan
Pitkin also claimed the three conspired to bring illegal gaming
equipment across state lines—more than one hundred thousand
bingo cards imported from Colorado.

"I have never had any payoff connections with police," a
bespectacled and balding Colacurcio, fifty-one, said of his first
federal indictment. "On the contrary, the police have been trying to nail me to the wall. . . . The next thing, they'll say I took a
lollipop from a kid." Besides, Frank added, the tolerance policy

was approved by City Hall. "Why would police have to be paid to maintain it? It's ridiculous."

Charged in a separate and bigger headline-making case was former assistant chief of police Milford E. "Buzz" Cook, who'd been a top assistant to now-retired chief Frank Ramon. Cook, who also briefly became police chief only to be indicted for perjury, denied knowledge of the police payoff system that he helped facilitate. During his 1970 trial, officer after officer took to the witness stand and testified about payoffs, giving some of the first public details on how the money moved through a system that dated back a quarter century and involved at least seventy officers. Cash flowed from club owners who were pressured to make payments or did so in order to operate illegally and maintain their monopoly, with the booty going to cops and to industry middlemen who pushed it up the line, doling out kickbacks of money, liquor, and other favors. Some cops were getting up to a $1,000 a month. Testimony was explicit, but much of it was unverified. One assistant chief, George Fuller, said he had "heard" that considerable cash had gone to City Council member Charles M. Carroll (known as "Streetcar Charlie" because of his former job with the old Seattle Transit System and no relation to prosecutor Charles O. Carroll). Pinball machines were licensed under a committee overseen by Streetcar, and he was already receiving thousands in campaign cash from the amusement industry.

Fuller said Streetcar, as a Council member, was reputedly getting $300 a month from a vice officer whose squad was sharing as much as $6,000 a month in payoffs. Vice cops kept payment records on index cards, with payees assigned code names. Those who didn't pay at the first of the month would be faced with drop-ins by beat cops who harassed customers, checking IDs and turning up outstanding tickets or warrants. The uniforms kept half what they were paid. The other half went to their sergeants, who kept half of that, and passed the remainder upward. Those at the top were getting money though different branches of the pipeline, leading to big monthly payoffs.

Among those testifying was Jake Heimbigner, owner of the Caper Club, a gay nightclub in the Morrison Hotel across from police headquarters, then on Third Avenue. He paid $165 in weekly protection money to stay open, he said. A police sergeant would call him and arrange meetings at various neighborhood locations where the payoffs would be made.

Beverly Grove, manager of Russell's Casbah Tavern and Cardroom on East Madison Street, said she paid $125 a month to the cops, then one day decided she'd had enough. Suddenly there was a lot of police work to do at the Casbah. Cops began ticketing customers for traffic violations and jaywalking, she said. "There isn't a customer in my tavern that hasn't been harassed," she testified. Her father, the tavern's owner, said a cop told him that bar work can be dangerous, and "I'm sure you don't want anything to happen to your little girl." Unable to make money, the Casbah closed.

Cook was convicted and went to prison in a tumultuous time for the SPD. Besides the corruption, the SPD was dealing with antiwar protests and bombings around Seattle. Rioting was an almost daily event in the early seventies, and demonstrators also took over Interstate 5. New mayor Wes Uhlman told a U.S. Senate committee there had been ninety explosive and incendiary devices set off from February 1969 to July 1970, damaging businesses, schools, churches, and private homes. Seattle ranked behind only New York and Chicago in the number of protest bombings and, per capita, ranked first. Police officers regularly worked twelve-hour shifts and routinely patrolled the streets six to a car, dressed in full riot gear. It was a war about war, with cops responding to demonstrator violence with beatings. In one University of Washington event, cops even covered up their names and badge numbers so they couldn't be identified in the assaults. More than three hundred brutality and misconduct complaints were filed in 1969 alone. Cops went from being called bulls; now they were pigs. SPD officers in return adopted a pig as a mascot and coined the motto "Pride, Integrity, Guts": PIGs.

Mayor Uhlman had just appointed an assistant chief, the respected Frank Moore, as top cop, when Moore too became tainted by the scandal, invoking his Fifth Amendment right before the U.S. grand jury. Moore then stepped down "due to his health." Uhlman began to bring in a series of outsiders, all California cops, to serve as interim chiefs. (Seattle would run through six police chiefs from 1969 to 1970: Ramon, followed briefly by Cook; then Moore, followed by Charles Gain, out of Oakland; Ed Toothman, also brought in from Oakland; and George Tielsch, from Garden Grove, California). The department discovered that as many as forty officers were involved in the payoffs, which appeared to have for the most part ended in 1968. Most of those named had already left the force. SPD officials asked prosecutor Charles O. Carroll to press felony charges against four officers who shook down businesses that catered to gays and lesbians, but he opted for misdemeanor charges and sought only suspended sentences.

Seattle attorney Christopher Bayley saw that as something of a cover-up and signed up to oppose Carroll for the prosecutor's job in 1970. A county grand jury could get at some of the illegal low-hanging fruit of the payoffs that a federal grand jury couldn't, he said. Bayley easily won the election, kicking out the embattled Carroll, a onetime University of Washington football star, after a twenty-two-year reign. As one of his first duties,

Charles O. Carroll, former Husky football star, was the King County prosecutor for twenty-two years. His record of public services was tarnished when he was linked with Seattle police bribery connected to gambling and other vice activities. (Photo: *Seattle Post-Intelligencer* Collection, MOHAI)

Bayley formed a grand jury that in 1971 indicted both Charles Carrolls—prosecutor Chuck and Council member Streetcar Charlie—along with seventeen others, including ex-chief Ramon, his former assistant Buzz Cook, and former county sheriff Jack Porter, for "conspiracy against government entities." Eventually, a hundred cops, many retired, were implicated in crimes that dated back thirty-five years.

Prosecutor Carroll's conspiracy role, the grand jury alleged, included being present at a meeting with pinball czar Ben Cichy and Sheriff Porter to figure out how to extend a tolerance policy countywide. It was a low point for Carroll, an All-American running back in 1927–28 and a 1964 National Football Foundation College Hall of Fame inductee. Most legendary was his 1928 college performance in a game against Stanford. Even though the Huskies lost 12-0, Carroll dazzled the crowd with such slash and dash that the *Stanford players* carried him off the field. President-elect and Stanford alumnus Herbert Hoover was so wowed, he exclaimed, "That man is the captain of my All-America team!"

Bayley later said he considered fellow Republican Carroll—whose county car was equipped with red lights in the grill so the prosecutor could dramatically speed to crime scenes—the closest thing to a local political boss. Carroll had dirt on almost everyone and used it to bend arms, Bayley said, adding, "He was called 'Chuck' by everyone, and 'Fair Catch' by critics who believed he never filed tough cases." Carroll had also been the first prosecutor to introduce the televised confession. Now and then he would show up on TV, sitting at a table with the suspect sandwiched between him and a deputy prosecutor. The perspiring suspect would explain how he did the awful crime, as Carroll nodded affirmatively for the cameras. Carroll not only scored campaign points, the dog and pony show was much cheaper than an actual trial.

Bayley also recalled how he visited Carroll "as a courtesy" to let the longtime incumbent know that he would oppose him in the 1970 primary. "He sat at the head of a long, polished conference table, flanked by his finance chairman and the Republican county chairman, all equally incredulous that he could be challenged by a thirty-two-year-old lawyer who had never tried a criminal case," Bayley said.

But once he dethroned Carroll and handed down the indictments, Bayley was on a downhill course. He was forced to drop some cases, including Streetcar's, while others were dismissed. By the time of trial in 1973, plea agreements and pretrial rulings trimmed the defendant list to ten. Ex-chief Ramon, who was alleged to have received liquor from operators of gambling establishments, got the charges against him dismissed before trial, after it was determined he'd testified before a grand jury under a grant of immunity.

Then King County Judge James Mifflin dismissed most of the remaining cases, including Carroll's. The evidence against the former prosecutor was particularly troublesome, the judge said. Carroll's accuser had admitted to some earlier legal run-ins and court appearances wherein he often lied under oath.

In April of 1974, the final defendant, a former cop, pleaded guilty to accepting bribes and was sentenced to two months in jail.

Chuck Carroll would later claim he never approved of the tolerance policy. "I said bring me the facts for a case and I'll file it. I always worried that there might be payoffs to permit the stakes to go higher and higher. And that's what happened. The names of some good people were dragged through the mud," including, he inferred, his. When Carroll died in 2003, prosecutor

Norm Maleng, the man who succeeded Bayley, said, "He was really a giant of his era, both in the sports and legal arenas. He was a grand old man, and I miss him. I really do."

The city's biggest corruption scandal had ended with a whimper, though Bayley felt it had changed the city. In a January 2007 op-ed piece he wrote for the *Seattle Times* on the fortieth anniversary of that paper's opening series on the shakedown system, Bayley said the indictments were at least a learning experience for the city.

"To this day I don't know how much Carroll knew about the payoff system. But he did not understand the degree to which press coverage of the tolerance policy had undermined his support from King County voters," he wrote. "Seattle finally began to understand how its legal and political system had been corrupted by years of payoffs . . . the grand jury and criminal trials exposed and effectively dismantled the system. Since then, Seattle police and local officials have had their share of controversy, but there has never been an allegation of [widespread] corruption. We forget those events at our peril. The recurring lesson is that government attempts to regulate human activity— be it drinking, gambling, drugs or whatever—must be based on public consensus and carried out transparently and openly. If there is no consensus, as with after-hours drinking in the '50s and '60s, there is an enormous temptation for police and public officials to 'wink' at violations, and the winking can easily devolve into corruption."

A few years back, Gordy Brock, one of the bar owners victimized by the police payoffs in that era, said in an interview, "The beat cops were bagmen, and I mean that literally. Every week, I put a paper bag on the bar. The beat guy comes in, sits down, has coffee, picks up the bag [with $100 cash] and says goodbye. In return, I don't get busted for code or liquor violations."

In 1949, at age twenty-one, Brock opened the Fremont Tavern (later the Red Door) and ran a number of places, including a rough bar on Capitol Hill where the lights occasionally failed. "When they came back on, everyone would be pointing a gun at everyone else," he said.

But it was the cops who really worried him during half a century in the business, winding up as owner, with wife Sandee, of the Pike Place Bar & Grill at the market. Until his 2001 death, at seventy-two, he was among the last of the old-time tavern keepers and payoff victims still in the business.

His cop bagman was never indicted, Brock said. In fact, he got full city retirement and hung around Bock's market bar for years afterward, working as a security officer and mooching drinks. It was some solace that post-tolerance mayor Wes Uhlman showed up to cut the ribbon at Brock's renovated Pike Place Market grill years later. "Still," Gordy said of the mayor, "I wanted to ask him for my money back."

Meanwhile, in the seventies, the feds were asking Frank Colacurcio to pay up. Which he did.

Betty Ballbuster

"The truth is, with my own eyes I never seen him working."

D ue to the relentless and inflammatory media coverage in Seattle, Frank Colacurcio got his gambling conspiracy trial moved to Spokane. It was 1971, and he was slowly being abandoned by his supposed codefendants. Bingo operator Harry Hoffman had a heart attack the night before the trial was to begin and was never able to testify. The other original defendant, Charlie Berger, operator of three bingo parlors, had defected to the prosecutor's side of the court. Also lined up against Frank were two of Berger's employees, bookkeepers Gilma Block and Betty Luke.

The frail, forty-two-year-old Luke, who was losing her sight, fighting alcoholism, and had suffered a mild stroke, was considered by some to be a bit of a heroine. After she agreed to testify against Frank, she had to have four U.S. Marshals watch over her when she received threats and obscene calls at her home. "It's been quite an education, at times a painful one," she said. "But I've been getting my education the hard way all my life."

Apparently two of Frank's attorneys thought a vacation would do her good. That resulted in federal witness-tampering charges being brought in 1971 against Richard Powers and James Alfieri. Betty Luke claimed they offered to pay her to leave the state to avoid being served with a subpoena to testify against Frank. They had to hire their own attorneys to save their necks and their bar cards. One of the hired mouthpieces was famed criminal defense attorney Anthony Savage, who once said, "You can't make any money in this business. That's why I play Lotto every week." But, like a moth to flame, he was attracted to losing causes: state senator John Bagnariol—convicted of taking a bribe in a political racketeering scandal called Gamscam—along with Seattle police detective-turned-extortionist Richard Bartlett, Cannery Workers Union murder mastermind Tony Baruso, cocktail lounge triple-killer Mitchel Stroy, and a throng of Indonesian dope smugglers and neo-Nazi members of the Order, the violent Jew haters led by white supremacist Robert Matthews, killed in a shootout and fire on Whidbey Island in the eighties. Savage also represented Green River murderer Gary Ridgway. He earned Ridgway a life sentence rather than a lethal injection through a plea deal that involved the killer's confession and detailing of forty-eight murders, many of them prostitutes he picked up and strangled.

Savage was the sort of guy, if you're guilty, you wanted grilling your accuser, as Savage did of the fragile Betty Luke.

"Why did you become a witness for the state?" he asked.

"It was my civic duty," Luke responded.

Savage wrinkled up his face.

"Pardon me," he said, "but I tend to gag on that one."

It was apparently effective: a jury acquitted both of Frank's attorneys.

Luke subsequently made a sort of testimonial tour of courtrooms in Seattle and Spokane. Among other accusations, she fingered ex-sheriff Tim McCullough as a bagman for the Lifeline Club, where she worked. She told how her club's revenue was skimmed to avoid taxes. She also detailed payoffs to officials and explained how gamblers and cops privately communicated by arranging secret meetings.

"I was so dumb for a long time that I thought payoffs were a legal and acceptable part of the tolerance policy," she said. "I mean that. When Mr. Berger went to McNeil Island Federal Penitentiary in 1965—he was there just six weeks—I ran things and it was natural to go ahead with the payoffs." Berger's clubs brought it up to $3,000 a day and sometimes up to $5,000 for special bingo events. An avid player might spend $10 an hour on cards, bought from a dozen saleswomen roving the floor, and win nothing, she said.

"What really got to me was seeing little old ladies—they outnumbered men by far—come in with their pension checks the first of the month and start playing. Some of them were cleaned out within a few days and they'd beg for loans to keep playing the rest of the month. It was considered smart business to advance them a little money because that kept them hooked."

In Spokane she blamed Frank Colacurcio for a lot of this, detailing his behind-the-scenes role of accepting payoff money from the bingo operations and then sharing it with cops who in return agreed not to interfere. Assistant U.S. Attorney Doug McBroom called Luke "the spark that started the whole investigation and successful prosecution of corruption in this city." She had been persuaded to do the right thing by Reggie Bruce, chief investigator for the state attorney general and the state Organized Crime Intelligence unit.

Among those who took the stand was former interim mayor Floyd Miller, who conceded the tolerance policy flew in the face of state law and that the gambling permitted at Berger's joint was illegal. Still, he said, apparently without irony, the policy "kept out Eastern gambling syndicates."

Miller also brought up the name of Al Rosellini. The ex-governor called up one day and "he just said the Lifeline Club and Berger were having a little problem," Miller testified. Rosellini merely "asked me to check it out." Rosellini had also contacted then-Seattle police chief Frank Ramon to ask about getting Berger's club reopened, it turned out. Ramon had said publicly he knew little about the club's operations. But Miller said Ramon told him he had undercover officers at the club. Others testified that Ramon's real contact at the club was former sheriff McCullough, who was directly involved in its operations.

Frank's brother Sam testified, too, only to say he didn't know anything. He didn't know how much Frank got when he sold his part in their former amusement business and had no idea what Frank might have earned running the Firelite Room, from where the amusement business was also run, and which in fact Frank didn't own. Their sister Frances Schmitz owned it, and they worked for her. Sometimes Sam would mess up filling in for Frank, he said, and his sister would even threaten to fire him. Furthermore, Frank did not own the bar at the Savoy, where go-go girls served drinks. That belonged to their other sister, Jessie Christiansen. By the way, Sam said, ex-sheriff McCullough, who ran for mayor in 1964, had a campaign based in the backroom at Ciro's restaurant, also run by Jessie. Most importantly, when asked if he'd ever seen bingo operator Charlie Berger give Frank "packages," like with money in them, Sam piped up, "Not once!"

Frank's sister Jessie later got up and corrected the record, saying it was she and Frances together who owned the Savoy. Either way, Sam and Frank were not involved. For that matter, she added, "I don't know anything personal about my brother's [Frank's] business. The truth is, with my own eyes I never seen him working."

Despite those familial testaments, but due in great deal to Betty Luke's bravado, Frank Colacurcio was found guilty on December 6, 1971, of his first federal law violation. He was convicted of five counts of racketeering for bringing illegal bingo equipment into the state. His ailing coconspirator Harry Hoffman was acquitted while the other onetime coconspirator Charlie Berger, who'd turned informant, was a free man walking, thanks to his immunity. "That was life in that time," Frank later recalled. "Say you were an operator in Seattle during the tolerance policy. You had a business, you had to go along with the show," he said. But "I've never paid off anybody for anything. I'm not a person who's going to be shook for any money."

Frank was sentenced to three years and a $6,000 fine. He staved off prison when a judge allowed him to remain free on appeal, only to become a campaign issue for his family friend, ex-governor Rosellini, who was trying to return to public office, challenging Dan Evans for the Olympia mansion.

Eight days before the 1972 gubernatorial election, the *P-I* ran a front-page piece citing links between Al and Frank— something Rosellini would later call "wop bating." The piece was written by executive editor Lou Guzzo (who'd go on to become an admirer, advocate, and biographer of a later governor, Dixy Lee Ray, who would appoint the semiretired Rosellini to the state highway commission). Guzzo, using no named sources, claimed Rosellini had helped one of Frank's brothers obtain a liquor license in Hawaii. The story led to suspicion over Rosellini's ties to organized crime, giving rise to bumper stickers stating "We Don't Need a Godfather."

In a 1997 authorized biography favorable to Rosellini, Frank is mentioned on just one of its 272 pages. The *P-I* report "tried to link Rosellini to a notorious local gambling and racketeering figure, Frank Colacurcio," the book states, downplaying Frank's long relationship with the governor.

Guzzo's article, printed without giving Rosellini any opportunity to respond, detailed a telephone call Rosellini had made on behalf of a relative of Colacurcio in 1968, when Rosellini was no longer governor, regarding a club license transfer in Hawaii. The article also recounted Rosellini's legal representation, in the distant past, of a Seattle bingo and club operator "purportedly" tied to Colacurcio. Hawaiian authorities had found nothing improper about Rosellini's contact in Hawaii, and Rosellini had readily acknowledged that in the 1940s, as a young lawyer and former prosecutor, he had represented the then-teenaged Frank Colacurcio on a charge of statutory rape. The Colacurcio family were longtime friends of the Rosellinis. . . .

Guzzo, years later, could not add any substance to his allegations, but he unreservedly stated his personal animosity toward Rosellini and his pride in the fact that his story "finally got Rosellini out of politics once and for all." Called a "baseless smear" by KING TV, the story was deliberately planted by Keith Dysart, a deputy to Attorney General Slade Gorton [later Republican U.S. senator], with the full knowledge of high operatives in the Evans campaign.

In an introduction to the Rosellini book, author Payton Smith wrote that he "frequently" encountered allegations that Rosellini was corrupt. "Whenever I could, I made it a point to track down the source. In three instances, I personally interviewed reporters who were reputed to have knowledge of these matters and in each case I learned that there was no verification for any allegations. . . ." He was satisfied, he said, that, had there been skeletons, "I would have found them." That was of course published six years before Rosellini would be implicated as a behind-the-scenes palm greaser in Strippergate, the Seattle political money-laundering scandal that led to felony convictions for Frank and son Frankie. Prosecutors said Rosellini, as part of Strippergate, delivered at least eleven checks to Council member Judy Nicastro, worth nearly $7,000 and signed by people who'd been reimbursed by Frank and Frankie.

It says something about Frank's notoriety that, as Rosellini and Guzzo both agreed, the *P-I* smear was the likely cause of Rosellini's 1972 loss to Evans. That was effectively the peak of Rosellini's storied political career. He was praised for improving and reforming the state's higher-education system, its adult and juvenile prisons and mental hospitals, the University of Washington Medical School, and the state's roadways—the Highway 520 Lake Washington floating bridge from Seattle to the Eastside was officially named the Governor Albert D. Rosellini Bridge in 1988. He continued to toil daily into his nineties, driving to work behind the wheel of a white Cadillac with the vanity plates GOV ADR. On the walls of his offices south of Safeco Field were photos of him with John F. Kennedy and Lyndon Johnson, who, it was rumored, had considered Rosellini as a vice presidential running mate in 1964. Rosellini worked at what he called his "consulting" business until he was forced to retire in 2008 due to his health.

At his hundredth birthday party in 2010, when asked for this book about his long relationship with Frank and the accusations that swirled around both of them, Al Rosellini said, "Just politics. Everybody, well not everybody, but many, on the opposition look for these things to criticize. I've never been concerned about it, because things happen in the world—sometimes all hell breaks loose. That's politics, and if you can't take it, you should get out of it. I am willing to stand up to any criticism."

At the party were current governor Christine Gregoire and five other former governors, including Dan Evans, who was sitting directly across the table from Rosellini. Thin and weak but mentally acute, Rosellini was in a wheelchair, disabled by a recent hip injury. Upon command, the other governors, including Evans, rose to help him blow out his century of candles. "We're all friends," said America's oldest living ex-governor, with a fine smile.

In a 1973 interview with the *P-I*'s Shelby Scates—cautiously headlined "Frank Colacurcio Interviewed"—Frank said he'd actually once been an Evans supporter but changed his mind because of the way Evans' state liquor board operated. "Those liquor inspectors can say what's lewd and obscene," he said. "They can close a man down. But what's lewd and obscene to one man isn't to another." He added: "I don't associate breasts with sex, but some people do. Other people associate hips with sex. It's all in the mind." He further stated: "I'm supposed to be the Mafia . . . Well if there's a Mafia here in this area, then Santa Claus is here for sure, too."

Frank remained defiant about his tax troubles, only to find the feds piling it on. In 1974, as he continued to remain free while his appeal for the first conviction wended through the courts, he was charged with evading another $87,510 in taxes for the years 1967 through 1969. The money was proceeds from such liquor and topless operations as the Firelite Room in Seattle and the Mirror Room at the Olympus Hotel in Tacoma, and from the George Investment Co., which owned the Olympus as well as the Tiki bar and eatery in Lakewood. His partners in the Tacoma and Lakewood businesses included brother Sam and brother-in-law Jim Schmitz, along with Seattle restaurateur Jim Ward, owner of the popular 13 Coins and El Gaucho restaurants. In the late sixties, Ward, the ostensible operator of the Mirror Room, lost his liquor license after inspectors determined he was fronting for Frank. At a hearing, Ward insisted Frank had no financial interest in the bar and was just "helping me with some of his experiences he had had and with some of the

Frank Colacurcio Sr., handcuffed between federal marshals, enters the U.S. Courthouse in 1973. He was convicted in 1974 of tax evasion, but the verdict was overturned on appeal. (Photo: Vic Condiotty/*The Seattle Times*)

specialists he had had in Seattle." Then someone showed him the joint Mirror Room bank account he shared with Frank.

Ward wouldn't be testifying at Frank's trial, however. He died in 1970. He fell dead while fishing on the Salmon River near McCall, Idaho. Just as questions had been raised about the 1969 drowning death of pinball king Ben Cichy in the midst of the Seattle corruption scandal, Ward's death raised eyebrows. The cause was said to be a heart attack, even though Ward was only fifty, and his doctor was among his fishing partners.

At his latest trial, Frank came up with a better defense strategy than in 1971: instead of glowering at the jury, he got up on the stand in the 1974 case and testified to his innocence. He tried to account for the disputed income by claiming to have included it under "miscellaneous" on his tax form. The reason? He didn't want the state to find out he owned the bars in question. He confessed to keeping their ownership secret— getting friends and relatives to sign the papers and take out liquor licenses in their names instead. As a convicted felon, he couldn't get a license. So, he claimed, an IRS agent had told him that it was kosher to report the money as undefined income.

With pencil in hand, Frank put on quite a show, testifying in open court for the first time in his life. He stood before a big money chart in the Seattle federal courtroom, outlining how he didn't break the law. "Whenever I had funds come in that I was unable to divulge," he said, "I'd mark them down on the books as 'ins.'" Whenever he had funds go out that he could divulge, they were marked in the next column, not surprisingly called "outs." At the end of each financial quarter, he'd carry over the difference between the ins and the outs. That amount became his "miscellaneous." That would be the figure he gave to Ethyl, his bookkeeper, who put it on the tax return.

The jury was unimpressed and convicted him of tax skimming. However, thanks to a legal technicality, Frank would later win on appeal, and the case was never retried. That's probably because the feds got what they wanted: that same year, 1974, Frank, who was "out," suddenly was back "in." He lost his long appeal on the 1971 bingo racketeering case and went off to the McNeil Island federal pen for twenty-five months. That helped open up the organized-crime market for others. Almost immediately, John Carbone began to expand his franchise in Pierce County.

Unlike in those earlier Tacoma hearings, Frank's name would come up publicly this time, and elected officials would take a tumble.

MOVING TARGETS

The Carboneheads

"You always wondered why, when you're out yachting, you would need to pack a gun."

In the seventies, a new round of corruption erupted in Tacoma, and Frank Colacurcio got a costarring role. The plot centered around a clumsy turf war waged by a gang known as the "Carboneheads," and if it had all been captured in a book, it would have had to be written by Jimmy Breslin, although some victims might not agree. "One of the U.S. attorneys called them 'The Gang That Couldn't Shoot Straight,'" bar owner Ron Chase said in an interview. However, he added, "I never saw it in that light. The gang didn't bungle the fire [at his tavern]. They destroyed the place." His wife, Pat, seconded that, recalling how Richard Caliguri, a stocky, thickheaded gangster from the John Carbone mob, crawled through a window of her Tacoma house one day and went straight to the kids' room. At five in the morning, he pointed a gun to the head of Pat's teenage daughter. "Don't move," he said, "or I'll blow your fucking head off." Caliguri stared at the teen's face. "I ought to kill you just because you look so much like your mother," he said.

Caliguri got the girl out of bed and had her tie up a girl-friend who was staying over while Pat and Ron were away. Known also as "Waco," which some pronounced "wacko," Caliguri was under the impression that the Chases ran their bar for absentee title holder Frank Colacurcio, although both the Chases and Frank denied that. Nonetheless, Caliguri and his bosses believed it, so he marched the Chases' daughter downstairs at gunpoint and picked up a butcher knife, which he first held to her throat and then used to slash the phone line. He left the girl unharmed, but with a message for her parents: "If they don't get out of the tavern business, they're dead."

John Carbone's Tacoma mob had much the same goal as Frank's: to control the flow of booze, sin, and corruption on their turf. But the Tacoma Carboneheads were reckless amateurs compared to the Seattle gang, a typical Second City act. "Most Tacomans know they can't compete with Seattle," television producer and author Paul LaRosa discovered in gathering material for his book *Tacoma Confidential*, "but what galls them, what has seeped into the city's soul over generations, is the way Seattle has beaten Tacoma at every turn for more than a hundred years." On the other hand, one of the few categories in which Tacoma could compete with Seattle was crime. Al Rosellini's fifties hearings exposed some of Tacoma's vast underworld, but let it smolder. The Carboneheads were pushing that history along with a series of assaults and arsons and the help of corrupt public officials. It was a pattern that would continue into the next century as well, when city and police officials conspired to cover up the actions of their sexually addicted and out-of-control Tacoma police chief David Brame, who, in 2003, murdered his wife, Crystal, in front of their children, then shot himself dead.

Frank Colacurcio was a silent owner or investor in some of the Tacoma and Lakewood bars targeted by Carbone, such as the Peking restaurant, formerly known as the Tiki. A topless bar for decades, it was destroyed by an arson fire in 1978. That was the same year Tacomans began to hear about other fires and men with flaming brooms.

A onetime used car dealer, "Handsome Johnny" Carbone graduated from rolling back odometers to opening topless joints, paying off cops, running prostitutes, and operating a corrupt bail bond business. The short, bespectacled Carbone, in his late fifties then, was a flamboyant dresser who'd just sold his 55-foot yacht, *Sea Tramp*, and was having a 65-footer built to replace it. The buyer of his old boat, for $400,000, was his mob lieutenant, Ron Williams, who choreographed Richard Caliguri's window entries and paid off cops with turkeys, hams, booze, and women. "It's hard to forget the guy," a Seattle Yacht Club member noted about Williams. "You always wondered why, when you're out yachting, you would need to pack a gun."

It was that kind of brilliance that characterized the Carboneheads' takeover of the bar business in South Tacoma and Lakewood. They attempted to burn down one rival bar by using flaming brooms to set its roof on fire. This was taking some time, and a lot of people driving past called police to say there were men running around a building and jumping into the air with brooms on fire. They dashed off before the cops arrived.

When brooms failed them, they resorted to Molotov cocktails. When that, too, failed, one moron told the other, "Use a thinner bottle."

The gang did get the fire going at their boss's house, however. John Carbone thought this would be a good way to earn insurance money and make himself look like a victim. With his $175,000 home in flames, he could pretend he was targeted by the same people who were torching taverns. When they asked him who did it, he could say "that Frank guy."

This did not go well. A detective went through the charred Gig Harbor house and when he got to the closet, he thought, "Arson." Carbone did not want his shoes to burn so he took them all out in advance, along with some of the better furniture and valuables. The detective also thought it was important that someone saw a moving van outside the boss's house the night before the big fire.

Investigators were instantly reminded of an earlier blaze at one of Carbone's own taverns, which he claimed some rival gang had set ablaze. The night before, a witness said, a big moving van had backed up to the tavern door and took away the beer and stools and every other good thing. Carbone seemed fortunate to always be relocating with the flames at his heels.

Altogether, the Carboneheads managed to torch ten taverns or businesses and four homes over a six-year period, with a $2 million loss. At one tavern, a guard was tied up and left to die in the flames, but escaped. Besides arson and murder threats, the gang performed insurance fraud and ran shakedown and protection scams, prostitution, and gambling.

It didn't hurt that Carbone had Pierce County Sheriff George Janovich on his side, paid to look the other way. The gang could commit crime with little worry or planning. Richard Caliguri had a free pass to go through anyone's window and threaten children, and his boss Ron Williams could destroy a competitor's bar and not look back. As Williams would later explain, giving testimony in a civil trial while he was being held in protective custody: "We would go down to the Players [rival club] and I would throw bottles, like a case of bottles, and break them up and throw them all over. . . . We would have cars impounded through various deputies for no reason at all. We worked through the bike clubs, bikers, the Shifters, we were giving them money to go down and be rowdy and start fights." If that wasn't enough, "We sent minors in. John Carbone got a hold of the liquor board and the sheriff's department and they raided the place, busted two minors, and got a violation."

Bribery was a necessary tactic to stay in business, he said. One former county licensing official, Williams recalled, "was a pretty heavy drinker. He would be in there—he always seemed to hit my place at the tail end of his drinking spree—and would want a girl. I would tell him, 'Pick a girl of your choice.' He would take her right out of the club, walk right out the door with her. I don't think we bought a license for a pinball machine, jukebox, dance license, throughout them years."

Even after the gang was indicted and locked up, along with Sheriff Janovich, some of the victims couldn't shake their fear that other Carboneheads were lurking. The Chases' topless-dancing tavern had been firebombed twice and would have been hit a third time had Carbone not hired an undercover cop to handle the torch. The Chases quietly moved their belongings to another residence, kept a gun by the bed, and drove home a different way each night. "You get so used to living like this for so long," Pat Chase said, "you don't know when it's right not to."

The thing about corruption, she added, was when it goes to the top, there is no one to help. Janovich was a lawman for three decades. After six years as a deputy out of high school, six years as a detective, and thirteen years as chief criminal deputy, he was elected sheriff by a 150,000-vote margin over the incumbent. A balding, rangy man who demanded loyalty and respect, he won praise for consolidating Tacoma police and county sheriff's record keeping, creating a canine unit, and drawing up the first mutual aid agreement for county law enforcement agencies.

Of course, he was a racketeer too. Federal prosecutors said Janovich ignored prostitution and other lawbreaking at the clubs owned by Carbone and Williams and at several others, independently owned, which catered especially to the military from Fort Lewis and McChord Air Force Base. Even as he campaigned for sheriff in 1974, according to court testimony, Janovich had reached a deal with the Carbones to make sure their bail bonding company got the cream of his jail's business by having jailers steer inmates to their office. In return, the Carbones gave tens of thousands of dollars to Janovich for his campaign and as living expenses.

Janovich's deputies also harassed the Carboneheads' rival club owners and made sure that arson investigations always hit dead ends. At Williams's suggestion, Sheriff Janovich steered suspicion in the shooting of state liquor agent Mel Journey away from the Carboneheads and toward other suspects. Journey was shot several times as he was getting into his car outside his Tacoma home in 1977, but survived. The two shooters were later identified by federal agents and convicted; they indeed had been hired by Williams. In a later confession, Williams said Carbone told him to have Journey killed or he, Williams, would be murdered. He also said Carbone got his instructions to kill Journey from Janovich.

The sheriff had to balance competing interests, however, according to court records. He was doing favors for Puyallup Indian tribal leader Bob Satiacum, who needed protection to sell illegal booze and cigarettes. Janovich reportedly told Williams, "You guys can have your topless business, the bail-bond business, your sauna bath business . . . [But] I don't want you going into the smoke shop business, the fireworks business, the Christmas tree business [that] Satiacum is operating."

Janovich also made sure Williams was tipped off whenever police planned to raid his bars. It was a protection racket that pretty much echoed Seattle's tolerance policy and also dated back to the fifties, except in this case the county's top lawman wasn't just looking the other way, he was directing traffic. In 1979, after a four-month federal trial, Janovich and five others were convicted of racketeering. Another six men earlier had pleaded guilty in the same case. Those sent to prison included John Carbone's son Joey and enforcer Caliguri, hit with an eighteen-year sentence. The piece of evidence that brought Janovich down was a tape recording, made by an undercover agent, of the sheriff accepting a $1,300 bribe. He was sentenced to twelve years but was released in six, having been moved from prison to prison about thirty times. Prisoners do not play well with the people who put them there. At age seventy-seven, still claiming he'd been wrongly convicted, Janovich died on Father's Day, 2005, from a ruptured appendix.

Gang boss Williams won freedom a few years later by cooperating with the FBI in the conviction of Indian leader Satiacum and providing information in other cases. His federal sentence was suspended, and a life term for a state conviction related to the attempted murder of Mel Journey was converted to immediate parole.

John Carbone spent fifteen years in prison and later, at age seventy-nine, died a feeble and demented old man at the mental hospital, Western State, down the road from where he'd burned his own tavern. He got a nice send-off in his hometown paper, the *News Tribune*, where someone with a short memory described him as "a simple guy. A good guy. Really."

The Carboneheads never got to where they were going, investigators said, but they were thinking big, planning to stretch their reach into Seattle. To that end, prosecutors said, they at one point planned to kill Frank Colacurcio. They got busted before they could get around to it.

Besides, they probably would have had to break into prison to get him.

Going Hollywood

"The guy's wiggling and screaming and saying,
'Don't drop me, I got the money, I'll give it back!'"

By 1978 Frank Colacurcio had returned to his Seattle bar
empire with the enthusiasm of most former inmates: where
are the ladies?! He steadily expanded his topless empire with new
venues and by the start of the eighties ran a handful of Seattle and
King County clubs and another half dozen scattered from the
Southwest to Alaska. At the moment, he was doing better than his
brothers at staying out of jail. Bill Colacurcio had gone off to run a
family-connected club in New Orleans, where he was convicted of
illegal gambling and racketeering, having bribed undercover officers who posed as corrupt cops. Brother Sam was running topless
bars in Arizona and in the family tradition also found his way to
the federal pen, convicted of skimming profits. He got four years
by plea-bargaining charges of conspiracy to commit bribery, theft,
and trafficking in stolen property at two clubs in Phoenix and one
in Tucson. Two other brothers, Patrick and Daniel, also pleaded
guilty to criminal charges connected to the Phoenix and Tucson
topless operations and did prison stints.

Not that anyone had forgotten Frank. A 1979 report compiled by the state patrol's Organized Crime Unit contended that
Frank controlled a "criminal organization" operating topless taverns and other businesses in the state, and looked like a good collar
for any jurisdiction with a well-funded vice squad. At a later legislative hearing on crime in New Mexico, a federal investigator testified that Frank's gang numbered about fifty throughout the West.
Through his exploits, Frank was providing full-time employment for task forces—and for writers, as well, including William
Chambliss. A sociologist and author, he wrote a popular 1978
book, *On the Take*, that delved into Seattle's organized crime and
tolerance policies. It was a generally accurate inside account, but
some questioned its precision. He refers to the Blethen family's
Seattle Times, for example, as a Hearst newspaper, and his account
of young Frank Colacurcio's rape conviction—at odds with the
court record—portrays Frank's plea as "taking a fall" in return for
a political deal arranged by his unnamed attorney (Al Rosellini):

> Frank was the son of a vegetable farmer in the county. His fam-
> ily was comfortable but neither notorious nor wealthy. He and
> some of his young friends were untouched by crime or rackets to
> any significant degree, but they were touched by the sin of many
> American men—womanizing. One of the women that Frank slept
> with regularly was only sixteen years old. She was also sleeping
> with several of Frank's friends. The young woman was arrested,
> and she confessed to the police that the older men had been hav-
> ing sex with her for some time. The police threatened all four of
> them with jail sentences. The four men denied the charge, and the
> police had only the uncorroborated testimony of the girl.
>
> A young lawyer who was active in politics managed the busi-
> ness affairs of Frank's family. The four accused rapists fell to
> arguing among themselves as to how to get out of the predica-
> ment. They called in the family's lawyer to mediate. The lawyer

contacted the police, who told him that someone had to stand trial. The police agreed, however, to drop charges on all but one of the defendants in return for a guilty plea. The lawyer took out a checklist and added up the pros and cons of having one of the four plead guilty to the charge. Some were married, some had businesses that would suffer; Frank was single and could afford the stigma. He was also only twenty-three, so the effect of having sex with a sixteen-year-old would look less awesome. The lawyer promised there would be no jail sentence, only probation or a suspended sentence. He also promised that when it was over the other men would put up the money to set Frank up in business.

The lawyer's power to negotiate a deal was less than he indicated it would be. He did get the charges dropped on everyone but Frank, but Frank had to spend eighteen months in the state reformatory. On release, however, the lawyer kept his promise and set Frank up with a liquor license, a tavern, and a going business, without Frank's having to invest any money.

Accurate or not, it contributed to Frank's legend as a mobster, and a ballsy one at that. On one occasion, Chambliss writes, "a leading politician called Frank in to put him in his place. According to someone who witnessed the encounter, when Frank entered the room, the politician said, 'I understand you are the biggest pimp in the state.' Frank replied, 'Yeah, and I hear you like to play with little boys.'"

That quote, though it may sound contrived, may more likely be true. One of Seattle's oldest vice rumors is that of high-ranking politicians having once been involved in a boy-sex ring. Reporters from the fifties into the nineties heard cops and others speak of it; the usual suspects included state and national politicos. Giving credence to such talk was the 1988 suicide of King County Superior Court Judge Gary Little, who took his life after learning that a story on allegations that he had abused children would be published in the next day's *P-I*. There had long been questions about Judge Little taking juvenile offenders to his home, while others claimed they were abused by him. In the *P-I* story, reporter Duff Wilson, now with the *New York Times*, revealed Little had been disciplined for inappropriate contacts with juvenile offenders by the state Commission on Judicial Conduct, but details had been kept secret. As the paper went to press, a courthouse janitor discovered Little's body in his chambers next to a gun and a suicide note:

> I have chosen to take my life. It's an appropriate end to the present situation. I had hoped that my decision to withdraw from the election and leave public life would have closed the matter. Apparently these steps are not satisfactory to those who feel more is required, so be it. I will say one final time that I am proud of my efforts and accomplishments as a Superior Court Judge. I am deeply appreciative of those who have wished me well these past few weeks.

In an interview over late-night drinks a few years later, a Seattle police detective and former ranking vice squad officer revealed he had "the file" on this rumored history of man-boy rapes by our elected leaders. "Names, dates, everything," said the detective, who'd been an extremely reliable source for earlier stories. He was willing to reveal the file, which—according to him—included undisclosed police investigations. The next day, his response was, "What file?" He couldn't seem to find it anywhere. Maybe in the end it was the ravings of a drunk. He had said he'd begun compiling the file because he might need it for "leverage" one day. As it turned out, the detective was later tried on theft charges and forced out of the department. If he had such a file, it didn't appear to have helped him in the job extortion market.

The mob lore about Frank naturally evolved into Mafia comparisons. Friends say he also seemed to fancy the role of

Hollywoodesque gangster from time to time. Take the night in San Francisco when he hung a man out a window, as the story goes.

"I don't remember his name," says a longtime Frank friend and business associate, "but the guy had made off with funds from the state Democratic Party. This was a big disappointment to the head of the party, who was Frank's old friend.

"So Frank goes to work and tracks the guy down in San Francisco. He finds him in a hotel room and, five stories up, opens the window and holds the guy out over the street by his neck. The guy's wiggling and screaming and saying, 'Don't drop me, I got the money, I'll give it back!' Which he did."

The incident amused Frank, says the friend, who understood how it grew his reputation. And it wasn't an isolated moment, says the friend, recalling another of Frank's tough-guy antics.

"One day we're sitting in the lobby of the Lake Quinault Lodge, by a big fireplace, talking business," he says, referring to the historic lakeside lodge on the Olympic Peninsula where Frank regularly went on wintertime fishing trips. "This was Frank's favorite place. He liked the setting, the quiet.

"So we're talking, and this woman comes up and starts looking at the coffee table between us. It's one of those wood-burl tables, for sale for $600. She sits down and rubs it and pokes around and starts asking about it. We don't know anything, we tell her.

"She sits there rubbing and poking, and Frank can't say what he wants to say [to the friend]. She won't leave. So finally he stands up, goes over to the hotelman, peels off six $100 bills, walks back, picks up the coffee table, and throws it in the fucking fireplace! The woman was running before her feet hit the ground."

The Mafia-accusation stories were a sort of running joke among Frank's friends. One of the reliable tales was the day Frank was waiting in court, when a cell phone, belonging to an investigator on his defense team, rang. The ring tone was the theme

Frank Colacurcio walks through downtown Seattle July 9, 1980, after facing arraignment at the federal courthouse on charges of conspiracy to evade income taxes. (Photo: AP/Wide World Photos/Gary Stewart)

from *The Godfather*. A friend insists another *Godfather*-inspired event is true as well—that Frank ordered a bloody horse's head be left in the bed of a prosecutor in the seventies. It could never be substantiated, and those who might know said they hadn't heard the tale even as a rumor. "No, it happened, they broke in and put the head in the guy's bed," the friend says emphatically. "The prosecutor never said anything about it publicly that I know of."

Frank is not Mafia, no way, the friend adds. "He has his own crime family. Literally."

Never much of a sinner in the smoking and drinking categories, Frank in his earlier days was typically polite in meetings with reporters or when turning down an interview that might convict him of something. "I don't want to be rude," he told one reporter, "but I have learned over the years to watch what I say to reporters and I would really rather not comment right now. I hope you understand."

In one eighties chat with a writer, over the pulsing music at the Firelite on Second Avenue, Frank was putting in a shift as bartender. He was a stocky rock of a man then, at 180 pounds, married for a quarter century to an understanding but distant wife. When he wasn't angling for money and women, he liked to fish in Alaska. He flashed a well-practiced angelic smile and sometimes kidded with strangers—at one of his federal tax trials, he stopped an IRS agent in the court hallway and asked if his new wool suit would be a deductible legal expense.

Frank talked animatedly if the subject interested him, and it did this night.

"That dancer over there," he said, pointing to a topless woman writhing under amber-colored lights on a mirrored Firelite stage, "that's a guy. Was a guy. Or is a guy, I don't know. Can't remember if he got the operation or is gonna get it. Look at the money they're throwing at him. He is one good-lookin' broad!"

A longtime Colacurcio associate recalls there were three pre-operative transsexuals or transvestites who danced as women at Frank's clubs. One became the object of affection of a local politician who was friendly with Frank. One night at the club, Frank and the associate spotted the politician (the associate wouldn't name him) sitting in a booth with the busty preop—the pol's face was smeared with lipstick. Frank was breaking up with laughter when the unknowing politico raced up to the bar and ordered more drinks for "me and my girl."

Says the associate today: "I told Frank to let me buy this round. Frank said no way! He had to have the honor. We never did tell the guy he was smooching another guy."

That night behind the bar, Frank repeated his mantra about being unfairly maligned as a "mobster." He was a businessman, in a business that attracts trouble and troublemakers, he said. That's all.

Thing is, as several of his associates point out, he was never satisfied with legally pocketing easy money. It was in his blood to find some way to cook the books and go to prison even when he knew the feds were watching. So nobody was surprised when, in 1981, only a few years out of prison, he got snared once more for skimming at two of his dance joints.

Then sixty-three, Frank and partner Kent Chrisman, forty, were charged with evading corporate income taxes at the Bavarian Gardens topless tavern in Bellevue and the Brass Tiger in Federal Way, among his first forays into the burbs. It was a near repeat of his 1974 case and, "Well, you know it is tough to beat a charge like that," a kind of hapless-sounding Frank allowed.

At his federal trial in Portland—his reputation almost guaranteed a conviction in Seattle, his attorneys said—prosecutors began dredging up the past that Frank said was all lies. They spoke in the superlative—kingpin, legend, empire—and told a jury how lackeys ran his operations because, as he admitted at his last trial, he couldn't get liquor licenses in his name. This time, partner Chrisman was the front man, said U.S. prosecutor Ronald Sim, and the twosome's accounting systems were "almost audit proof," the key word being "almost."

Frank's attorney portrayed him as the victim of government harassment, and codefendant Chrisman insisted he was the owner; after all, he was the guy who gave away free beer to everyone, including any member of the Seattle Seahawks, who showed up regularly. Frank, he said, was merely a consultant to whom he paid $200 a month. But the evidence was staggering: five thousand financial documents and the testimony of insiders who described how bar records were altered or destroyed so that Frank and his partner could hide cash profits—$150,000 from one bar alone—and avoid paying taxes. One witness was worried about his health. "I don't want to discuss anything," he said. "I got my bod to worry about." The former and present employees and dancers who did talk it up on the stand were described by Frank's attorneys as thieves, drug users, and mental cases. In some instances, that may have been true. But the feds had the goods on Frank and threw in a few other trade secrets to boot. The "booze" that customers bought for dancers was known as "lady drinks" and was, in fact, sodas costing $3 a pop. And those "Amateur Nights" at the taverns, when anyone off the street could dance topless to win a prize? They were Frank's dancers who came over from one of his other clubs. Frank's Talents West agency also provided dancers to competing topless taverns as well, for a $500 monthly fee.

Among those who testified, reluctantly, in Portland against Frank was his former Bavarian Gardens manger, Gilbert Pauole. A convicted heroin dealer, he and Frank had shared a cell at McNeil Island, and Frank later hired him as a doorman and bouncer before making him a manager. "I look at Frank

Colacurcio as my dad, my friend, and a very special person," Pauole said during the trial. Frank was godfather to his son as well and had given Pauole a necklace with a gold charm shaped like a pepper, a symbol of his trust in Gil.

The feds made their case nonetheless, and Frank was convicted of conspiracy and tax fraud. In 1982 he was given four years in a Texas federal prison. He was sixty-five. Time to think of retirement.

But even before he was released from the Fort Worth pen, the feds and others were anticipating his return. Nothing had changed in Frank's world, according to an IRS agent who appeared behind screens to conceal his face during 1985 crime hearings in New Mexico's capital city, Santa Fe. Daryll Whitehead, who would be on Frank's trail for years, said Colacurcio was piping orders to others who visited him in prison, and they had begun expanding into New Mexico. Whitehead, who had testified at Frank's latest trial, told the Governor's Organized Crime Prevention Commission that Frank, even while in prison, had taken over two Albuquerque bars—the Palomino Club and the Chapter 11—where, most likely, he was skimming profits. Typically, Frank moved in on financially troubled bars, offered to help them bring in topless dancers from his Talents West agency in Seattle, then ended up wresting control of the bar, Whitehead said.

Asked about all this, Frank's Seattle attorney William Helsell said it wasn't true. His client was a model prisoner, working in the kitchen, and was likely to serve every day of his term. "If the parole board treated him like everyone else, he'd be out by now," said Helsell.

"They're pretty unsympathetic to poor Frank."

Chinatown

"They do a few crimes. They get away. They do a few more. They get away. Then a murder. They're on their way."

It was during Frank's latest incarceration that three young Asian men entered the Wah Mee private gambling club off Maynard Alley in Chinatown on the early morning of February 18, 1983, as Seattle's most tragic vice-related crime began to unfold. They put on their gloves, took out their guns, and turned the day into Seattle's worst mass murder: thirteen dead. The Wah Mee club had thrived during the tolerance policy days, when winners could take home a $1,000 pot from one of the Pai Kau and mah-jongg betting games, with the house taking its 5 percent. It continued to exist in the eighties because of a City Hall attitude to not spend much time going after Chinatown's mostly harmless late-night gaming and bottle clubs—where members brought their own booze to be served up to them—and because the police force had few Asian members who could get in on the secretive action.

The Wah Mee ("Beautiful China") was once called Blue Heaven, writes historian Todd Matthews. "As its [earlier] name implied, it was a place for dancing, drinking, gambling, and partying. The Wah Mee Club's roster of members had always been a 'who's who' of the Asian community. . . .

> Around the gaming tables, gamblers sat with grim faces, swapping stories while concerned with the matter at hand: winning and winning big. The Wah Mee thrived, but problematically. It endured several "rashes" of crackdowns over several decades, usually when new mayors were seeking the seat of incumbents and bringing to the forefront a gambling tolerance policy that had existed in the city of Seattle for nearly a century. The Wah Mee grew cautious of its members and began to lean more toward patronage that consisted of family associations, tight-knit circles, and select tongs—a patronage limited essentially to Chinese members who knew the management. Eventually, the Wah Mee Club went "underground."

By 1983 security ruled. A guard sized up guests through a peephole into Maynard Alley, and another guard rechecked them as they came through a set of steel doors and down the stairs to a pastel Chinese parlor of tables, chairs, and a bar. The place was wired with a warning buzzer and panic alarm to alert mangers to intruders. Yet street thugs Willie Mak, twenty-two, and Benjamin Ng, twenty, the primary gunmen, had played at the club before and knew how to get in. On February 18, bringing along a third man, Tony Ng, twenty-six—no relation to Ben—they launched a plan to rob the fourteen people inside, mostly Chinese restaurant owners and employees. Mak and Benny Ng, at least, did not intend to leave any witnesses, and once they entered the gaming area, they raised their guns, ordered everyone onto the floor, tied each one with their hands behind them, and proceeded to shoot them all. Some waited in agony for their moment to die as the killers walked around and methodically shot each player one by one. They brought along no masks to disguise their faces, only surgical gloves to hide their fingerprints.

Tony Ng had thought it was just going to be a heist; he had originally agreed to go along to help repay a $1,000 debt he owed Mak. But the day before the shootings, Ng got the money from his girlfriend and tried to back out. He didn't want any part of the robbery. Mak refused. Well, Ng said, he just might go to the police then. Mak fired a warning bullet into the floor, telling Ng he'd kill him—along with his family and girlfriend— if he did. "Now go home," Mak added. "I'll pick you up later. If you're not home, I'm going to kill you."

Willie Mak and Benny Ng had been a two-man Chinatown crime wave for almost a decade, starting in the seventies. Mak liked to shoot at barking dogs and fire wildly out the window from his moving car. After the massacre, it came out that the two were connected to three other murders and were involved in numerous assaults, robberies, burglaries, and rapes. Ben Ng, with an uncontrollable temper, once set his girlfriend's cat on fire in her bathtub. He also shot and killed a seventy-one-year-old jogger, Franklin Leach, who happened to run past Ng and Mak while they were dumping a safe, taken from a burglary, in Lake Washington. The year before, 1982, two Chinese women, Lai Lau, forty-five, and her mother, Lau Chung, seventy-one, were killed by two Seattle robbers. A witness who came forward after the Wah Mee shootings said the women's killers were Mak and Ng.

Two weeks before Wah Mee, Ben met with the leader of Hop Sing Tong Association, one of Chinatown's many secret, but usually peaceful, societies. Within the Hop Sing, however, there was another secret society, led by a self-styled godfather. A person who attended the meeting heard the godfather make a special offer to Ng for his rite of passage from adolescence—he had just turned twenty.

"I can sell you a bulletproof vest," the godfather said.

Ng shook his head. He didn't need protection.

"I shoot people," he said. "People don't shoot me."

At Wah Mee, with everyone hog-tied, Ng even argued with Mak over how to shoot people.

"Let me kill them with the big gun," Ben said, referring to a large-caliber weapon they brought along. Willie said, "No. It makes too big a noise. Use the small one." He handed over his small gun, and Ben went to work.

Not much moved them. After the Wah Mee shootings, Ben went home to bed, and Willie went bowling.

"You don't look at the end, you start at the beginning," then-prosecutor and later Superior Court Judge William Downing said in an interview, reflecting on the evolution of Mak and Ng from misdemeanants to mass murderers. "They do a few crimes. They get away. They do a few more. They get away. Then a murder. They're on their way. Everything builds up to that day," Wah Mee. "In that respect, it's not an unusual story."

But while thirteen would die that morning in 1983, the fourteenth victim, a man named Wai Yok Chin, sixty-one, was only wounded. Like the others around him, face down on the floor, he lay silently after the barrage of bullets, bleeding from the slugs that tore into him. Hoping he might survive, Chin concentrated on what his assailants had looked like, and in his mind began to reconstruct the crime. Once the trio left with the money, Chin stumbled out the door and was able to relate information to police that led to the arrests and—later, thanks to his testimony—the convictions of all three. He later wondered if he'd been protected by a lingering family spirit: his brother, once a bartender at Wah Mee, had died in the same room years earlier from a massive stroke. In 1993 Wai Chin died at age seventy-one. It was, his family said, from natural causes.

Mak, the ringleader and main shooter, was sentenced to death—a sentence later overturned. Like Ben Ng, he is now doing life without parole. Tony Ng, who did no shooting, was convicted of thirteen counts of first-degree robbery but acquitted of murder. That left open the possibility of parole, and three decades later, he may be on the verge of it. A small crowd showed up for his 2009 parole hearing, asking that he not be released, ever. Some talked about the alleyway as a disturbing, ongoing force in their lives. Community member John Lew said he always thinks of that long-ago scene inside whenever he passes the old club site. To him, it is a haunting blemish, "not just for the families in this room, but it's a blemish [for] the whole Chinese community." Others still lamented the original jury verdict that absolved him of murder.

Tony Ng's attorney John Muenster had told the jury at his trial, "All evidence shows that, fundamentally, [Tony] is a decent person. The prosecutor seeks to brand him a murderer because he yielded to fear." And juror Diann Fouse told reporters then, "We felt he was under duress for being in there in the first place. I believed Ng's testimony. I don't think he lied. That's my gut feeling." Members of the state Indeterminate Sentence Review Board seemed to now share some of that sentiment. In 2010 they opened a path for Ng's release.

"It is the board's unanimous decision," read the ruling, "that now is the time to parole Mr. Ng to his final count," meaning he could be reviewed for release on a regular basis starting within four years. "Mr. Ng has admitted that his participation was due to bad decisions that he made," stated the ruling. "He is now described as a person who can ask for help and who understands the impact that his actions have had on an entire community, including his own family."

The victims' families, remembering the impact on them, hardly agreed. Arguably, as the jury decided, Ng's role was mitigated by his own horror at what was happening when the shooting began. And perhaps he'd done the necessary time for the crime: thirty-some years for robbery. But "bad decisions"? It seemed a less than artful description of what happened on the Wah Mee's killing floor and a thin rationale for Tony Ng's possible return to society in 2014. "The sadness hidden in me all of a sudden came out, worse than a flood," said one family member, Lin Yee Yock Wong, to the board. "I want to ask the offender, 'Do you still dare to ask for parole and release?' That's a shame."

Others said they were still shocked that nice Seattle would have such people as the Chinatown killers.

But the city has its aberrations. Take the guy who killed thirty-eight Mafioso.

Mafiaworld

"I killed my first man when I was sixteen years old. I just walked up behind him and blew the top of his head off. He was dead before he hit the sidewalk."

Frank continued serving his time in prison—he'd do three years altogether in the early eighties—and while authorities were convinced he was the head of local organized crime and would return to his old ways, it seemed clear he was not Mafia, depressing as that may be. "I hate to disappoint the Chamber of Commerce," author Gay Talese commented several decades ago as his limousine sped down Fifth Avenue in Seattle, beneath the monorail, rushing to another book interview, "but Seattle is just not a Mafia town." He guessed there could be two Mafioso around, give or take one, and they would be here only in retirement or hiding. Talese seemed to be in a good position to know. He'd just completed *Honor Thy Father*, his inside account of the Bonanno crime family, headed by Sicilian-born Joseph Bonanno, aka Joe Bananas. "It's odd," Talese added, "but people seem almost disappointed when you tell them the Mafia is centered in New York, Chicago, Detroit, and not in their city. Violence is part of our nature and because of it, people get a vicarious thrill out of the Mafia, although they probably won't admit it."

Even Frank always appeared to be amused by the allegations he was Mafia and indeed connected to the Bonanno family. State investigators had reported in the seventies that he met in Yakima with Joe's son, Salvatore "Bill" Bonanno. Investigators said the two got together and discussed a possible business relationship, perhaps a turf agreement or plans to share financing of some topless dancing ventures. When a reporter later asked Frank if he'd met with Joe Bonanno's son, he admitted only that he had gone to Yakima to gather up some produce. He picked some hot peppers, Frank said, "but I didn't pick no bananas."

Bill Bonanno had his own history around here, having done time at McNeil Island when it was a federal prison. His father ran one of the New York families from 1930 until he was nonviolently deposed in 1964, later dying of natural causes in Arizona. His gang became the Carmine Galante organization until Galante was deposed by gunfire at Joe and Mary's Italian-American Restaurant in New York City. Philip Rastelli took over only to be deposed by prosecutors and sent to prison. Today, the family has an "acting boss," according to the feds: Salvatore "Sal the Ironworker" Montagna, who, with underboss Nicholas "Nicky Mouth" Santora, bosses perhaps 130 made members. Like the other four major New York families, the organization has watched the bottom fall out of the crime market, the mob increasingly losing share to street gangs. The families today seem to exist more in books and movies than in life.

The younger Bonanno worked both sides, a Mafioso who became a writer and producer of TV films about his family. In the sixties he survived an attempted hit—fifty shots were fired, and all missed. That launched a mob feud known as the Banana War. He and his father negotiated a peace agreement that included

Joe's early retirement. For a twelve-year spell, while involved in organized crime, Bill toured various prisons, including a thirty-month stretch at McNeil for probation violation. There he read stories about organized crime in Washington state, including the Carbonehead gang scandal that brought down the sheriff of Pierce County, and it made him laugh. "I realize to you who live here, all this is traumatic," he told a reporter who asked for his perspective. "Well, this is not news. This is old stuff."

Still, there is a good sprinkling of mob vice-related history in Seattle and around the state by made members who practiced their art mostly under assumed names. Former New Jersey mob informer Nicholas Mitola Jr., who was in the witness protection program under the name Michael Milano, killed a man in 1991 at a Spokane card room. Mitola, who had testified against twenty members of the Lucchese crime family in the eighties, pleaded guilty to manslaughter and got a mere four years in prison. The family of the victim, George Vedadi, later sued the federal government for failing to properly supervise Mitola. "Spokane," said attorney Carl Maxey, "has been used almost as a primary location for many people in the federal witness protection program. It's very evident that there's a question whether they're well-supervised while they're here."

Some came to live in peace. Virginia Hill, the girlfriend of mobster Bugsy Siegel, who was killed in a fusillade of bullets at her Beverley Hills home in 1947, later married and moved to Spokane. But after she testified before the Kefauver Committee organized crime hearings in 1951, she wound up in tax trouble, and the IRS auctioned off all her Eastern Washington property. From there she left the United States for good. In 1966 she died from a drug overdose in Austria.

Paddy Calabrese was a mob informant and protected witness who became a private investigator in Seattle. A onetime

Mafia gunman who robbed Buffalo City Hall, Calabrese's life was made into a 1980 movie starring James Caan, called *Hide in Plain Sight*. After testifying against New York mobsters, he and his wife and children were unsuccessfully sought by Mafia killers. He, too, lived awhile in Spokane under an assumed name and ran the Sherlock Holmes Cafe and Precinct House. His financial backer was a local cop. He moved to Seattle and opened a Pioneer Square private investigations firm in the late eighties, specializing in tracking down unfaithful lovers. Typical was the case of a Chicago woman who apparently had been dating the same man as a Seattle woman. "She wanted to find out, you know, talking about the jealousy aspect area," he said. "I mean, she just wanted to see what the Seattle woman looked like, if she was better looking than her or something. I get this all the time."

Among the best-known local mobsters was Henry Hill, the onetime FBI informant who wound up living in a Seattle suburb. A Lucchese crime family associate whose life was immortalized by Nicholas Pileggi in the best-selling book *Wiseguy*, then depicted by Ray Liotta in the 1990 Martin Scorsese film *Goodfellas*, Hill, wife Karen, and their two kids joined the witness protection program and lived first in Nebraska and Kentucky, then in Redmond. They occupied a five-acre spread and survived on $1,500 a month in witness money. An alcoholic and druggie, Hill was busted for cocaine trafficking in Seattle in 1987 under the name Martin Todd Lewis. A prosecutor said Hill didn't actually complete the $10,000 drug deal, staged to go down with a vice informant in Kirkland, because he was "so screwed up on cocaine." Hill was divorced two years later and was booted out of the protection program for running up a new string of crimes. He has since remarried a family friend who once shared his addictions. He lives in California, starring in documentaries about himself. But he still battles the bottle. In December 2009 the sixty-six-year-old ex-mobster was in the St. Louis area for a showing of his artwork at a Larry Flynt strip club and, after getting involved in a drunken disturbance, was taken away in handcuffs. "I don't remember too much," he said, "I drank just one too many. I woke up a few hours later in a jail cell."

Vincent "Fat Vinnie" Teresa, once the number three man in the New England mob until he, too, became a government informant, died in a Seattle suburb in 1990. He had lived in Maple Valley near Renton under the name Charles Cantino after his testimony in the seventies led to the indictment of more than fifty mob members, including Meyer Lansky, the architect of organized crime's gambling and money syndicates (and the father of Paul Lansky, a West Point grad and former Air Force captain, who lived a respected life in Tacoma). In the eighties Fat Vinnie was indicted in Seattle on charges of smuggling rare birds into the country, pleaded guilty, went to prison, and later returned to the Seattle area in full retirement. The cause of his death, at sixty-one, was kidney failure.

Ex-Mafioso Lawrence "Sal" Iorizzo, who was running fuel scams around Seattle, was busted in Bellevue in 1995. He made more than $200 million for the mob working gasoline-sales rackets elsewhere, evading taxes and laundering the money. After he testified against fellow mobsters, he slipped into the witness protection program, then was kicked out for committing more crimes and went on the run. It was unclear how long he'd been in Bellevue, but he was shipped off to Houston for trial and his return to prison.

Most memorable was ex–Mafia hit man Max Kurschner, who spent six months maintaining a low profile at a South Seattle apartment in the eighties before authorities caught up with him on a tax charge. His alias was Joey Black, and he was an author of crime books under that name. In one, he wrote:

> I killed my first man when I was sixteen years old. I just walked up behind him and blew the top of his head off. He was dead before he hit the sidewalk.

That would have been 1948. By 1973 he had worked himself up to thirty-eight killings, all but three of them contract hits for the Mafia. The three others were revenge, he wrote.

> They came into the house looking for me and when they realized I wasn't home, they got abusive. One of them kicked my wife in the stomach and they left her lying on the kitchen floor. She started hemorrhaging. She was dead by the time our neighbors got her to the hospital.
>
> I started to hunt them down. . . . I found the first one in California. I killed him very slowly . . . I just started to pump bullets into him methodically. First into his rib cage so he would bleed. Then into his shoulders and then I shot his ears off. I just kept reloading the gun; I was having a good time.

At least some of his account seemed true. Kurschner said he had been investigated for seventeen murders—he had actually performed only three of those particular killings. He was never convicted of any of his hits, the difference being he was a killer who killed killers. His victims were other hit men.

The *Seattle Times* wrote about his arrest and past, and, after he was sealed up in McNeil, being held temporarily on the tax charge, he called up the *Times* reporter.

"Don't write about me anymore," said Kurschner, a stocky and mustachioed Yosemite Sam type. "Leave me out."

That spawned another story. When he got out of prison, he called up the reporter again, saying he was thinking of killing him.

"I'm sorry," he corrected himself. "I'm not going to kill you. That's against the law. I'm just going to take away little pieces of you until you don't exist."

All journalists are accustomed to disgruntled readers, and the rule is not to worry about the killers who call you up so much as the ones who don't. Kurschner liked publicity—he had at one point been on NBC's *Today Show* promoting one of his books, claiming he made and spent roughly $4 million gambling, drug-peddling, hijacking, and murdering.

Nearing fifty, he was feeling a little vulnerable and came here to vanish and, most of all, not to have the world know that Max Kurschner was Joey Black. The *Times* stories in the eighties put a crimp in his retirement plan. They also led to renewed interest in some of his killings. A San Francisco private detective, for example, was trying to connect Max with the killing of a Mafia squealer. Joe "The Baron" Barboza was a hit-man-turned-informant whose testimony implicated Frank Sinatra in Mafia business and helped put New England crime boss Ray Patriarca in jail. Barboza was shotgunned from a passing car in San Francisco in 1977. The private eye was working for Gennaro "Gerry Lang" Langella, acting boss of the old Gambino crime family, who was accused of ordering the hit on Barboza. The detective was trying to shift blame toward Max instead.

It turned out Kurschner had told Seattle TV reporter John Sandifer that he indeed had done the Barboza hit. "On the basis of what Max told me," Sandifer said, "there were two guns in on that killing. Max and a sideman." That was of little help to Langella, however. He was convicted and sentenced to life in prison.

Meanwhile, the *Times* told police about Max's threats to their reporter. The cops in turn sent a couple detectives to see him and explain how the phone threats could have a poor effect on his parole.

That didn't work well either. "Hey, so you called them down on me," he said in his next call to the reporter. "Hey punk, I never said I was going to kill you. I never used that word. I just want to fight you fair and square. You name the time and the street corner."

Kurschner said he'd catch up with the reporter soon. But somebody else resolved the issue. Months later, Max, forty-nine, had arrived in the Bay Area for what turned out to be a brief stay at a San Mateo motel. "Then Wednesday night someone came up and said good-bye with a shotgun," said a San Francisco journalist. "The cops figure it's a gangland killing." Someone had walked up, like Joey Black had in his first kill, and blew the top of Max's head off. As he lived, he died.

Speaking of legends, Madam Rose Marie Williams never killed anyone. But what a way to go.

Prostitution Reigns

"I've got men who give me $15,000 here, $10,000 there.
I shoot for the moon."

The record is unclear whether Frank Colacurcio and Rose
Marie Williams had any kind of working relationship, but
they operated in similar ways—getting out of jail and going
straight back to work—and they ran in the same circles. When
first arrested in the late sixties for running a call girl ring, Williams had a little black book that was rumored to include names
of some of Seattle's leading citizens: judges, politicians, and corporate execs. But following her guilty plea, the book was sealed
in a court file—by a judge—where it remains locked away today.

Just as Colacurcio-connected madam Ann Thompson had
ruled the prostitution market along with Nellie Curtis in the
fifties, Rose Marie began her rise to acclaim as Seattle's beauty
queen-turned-prostitute in the sixties, reigning as Madam
Washington into the next century. The five-foot-seven brunette
had been crowned Miss Washington USA in 1958—her hobbies included skiing, swimming, and sewing. A distant neighbor
to Frank at the north end of Lake Washington, she too would

prove to be an enduring police target. The onetime $300-an-hour madam had become legendary and seemingly invincible—frequently busted but rarely convicted, each time wiser to the ways of caution. She expertly insulated her operations and screened customers to ferret out undercover officers. She operated out of hotels, apartments, and parlors, as well as her home in a tree-shrouded neighborhood near Bothell. It was not until the nineties that law enforcement finally began to concentrate on ending the Rose call girl era. Continuing to operate as a prostitute and madam for decades, she was almost daring them to catch her. So for more than seven years, police focused on Williams's businesses, arresting and turning some of her female prostitution workers into criminal informants, and sending in male undercover cops willing to get naked in the line of duty. Police denied that officers actually had sex—if you don't define sex as getting your penis rubbed with oil, as one cop's was. At least two civilian police informants involved in making cases did have sex, one of them repeatedly for almost a year. Police never disclosed the details or said whether taxpayers paid the informants for their hard work.

By the late nineties, police felt they had enough evidence to go to court. Prosecutors brought both criminal and civil charges that included the likely confiscation of all of Williams's properties. According to documents presented to King County Superior Court, Rose attracted some of her clients by advertising in the dependable classified pages of *Seattle Weekly*, where sexual innuendo was a marketable commodity—and usually not just innuendo. Her in-call and out-call businesses included Karen's Personal Services, Touch of Magic, and Ambiance Massage/Escort Service. The latter allegedly was run out of a third residence Williams had an interest in, near Seattle's Green Lake. It was located in a residential neighborhood but had one feature other nearby homes lacked: white wrought-iron security bars covering all the doors and windows. There was also an array of security lights, and the address was posted in three places on the front and back of the house.

It was at that home, watched over by police, that sex workers were schooled on topics such as how not to get caught. They were informed, for example, on how to check a john's true identity. If an escort was called to a hotel, she should look "for medicine prescriptions, business cards, luggage tags, [or] airline tickets that indicate the customer is not a police officer or a 'bad trick.'" Prostitutes, who got to keep half of a $200 sex fee, sometimes talked in code to regular customers. "Dessert" understandably was intercourse, although "tea and crumpets" of all things was masturbation. "She said that if I thought they were a cop," one sex worker said, referring to Rose's dozens of male clients, "not to say anything, just leave—that if the man starts the conversation out by saying, 'So I get a blow job for X amount of money,' then they would probably be a cop." According to the women, regular code-knowledgeable customers who asked for "XYZ" got intercourse for $300. If they asked for "ABC," they got "the basic package . . . a Jacuzzi or a shower and a deluxe nude massage and a hand job" for $200. The madam did much of her own customer screening. Typically, after a grilling about marital status and work, "Williams asked me if I was a police officer," recalled one of the customers who stripped naked and paid $200 for a sexual massage at her home brothel. The split-level residence/bordello was across the street from her own family home in a manicured neighborhood that includes a grade school, whose parking lot she used for her customers, police said. "I told Williams that I was not [a cop]," recalled the customer. "Williams commented that 'You just never know.'"

But Rose's instincts failed her after all those years: one of the prostitutes she instructed on how to beware of cops was herself a cop—a King County Sheriff's undercover vice detective named Ruby, who was hired by Williams's sex operation, Karen's Personal Services. Detective Ruby gave at least one massage, apparently nonsexual, in the line of duty. And the customer who denied being a cop was one too. Mike, a King County vice detective, got fondled by Williams on his first visit to Williams's downstairs massage parlor. On his second visit, Mike pulled out only his badge and arrested her.

Among items discovered in a police search of the homes were three phone-answering machines, four caller-ID boxes, and an assortment of sex toys, condoms, dildos, a whip, and a riding crop. A $60,000 stash of $100 bills was found by cops in a safety deposit box. Her business could take in as much as $900 a session, police said. One customer, according to vice records, spent that amount over three hours and required a few extras such as a feather, a mirror, candles, and a scarf for him to wear.

Williams claimed the charges were untrue. "They claim to have taken down all these license numbers of men going in and out of the house. Those were my son's teen friends, visiting, nothing else. The police were outside watching, writing down license numbers!" And the money? "I made my money in restaurants," she said, "and kept it around in cash."

In 2000, after pleading guilty and avoiding a public trial, the madam went perfunctorily to jail. She was given ten days behind bars, fifty days of home detention, and ordered to do 240 hours of community service in return for a guilty plea to felony money laundering and promoting prostitution. Though she faced losing all her assets, worth nearly $1 million, she ended up forfeiting only the $60,000 under the plea deal, along with profit from the forced sale of the brothel across from her suburban home. The loss came to more than $200,000, likely the largest penalty ever rendered in a local prostitution case.

Who were her clients? Just like years earlier, when a judge sealed her black book, a Rolodex of apparent clients was never revealed, because of her guilty plea. By law, customer names were deleted from police files released to the press, and Williams said there was "nothing in that [Rolodex] but my friends and associates." In a court statement, one of the sex workers described them as mostly "older gentlemen, married, most of them range from [their] late twenties all the way to sixty-something . . . well-to-do clients, you know, important men. One has known her since high school. One of the gals who worked for her met an older gentleman and [is] now driving around in a Mercedes." She added: "Rose sort of puts me down [for] being stupid [because] I'm not getting everything I can from a man. She mentioned, 'I used to be in this business when I was young like you. You know, I've got men who give me $15,000 here, $10,000 there. I shoot for the moon.' That's her exact words to me. In her eyes . . . men are money."

During court proceedings, the bobbed and bespectacled Williams—her looks aided by plastic surgery, according to ex-employees—had little to say other than that she had been through a lot. The madam's attorney claimed she'd been inactive as a prostitute for years until, while working as a legitimate masseuse, she simply relapsed when someone made a too-tempting offer. A grim Williams seemed embarrassed and distraught. In interviews with detectives, some of her ungrateful former sex employees called her an intimidating and "mean . . . very mean" boss, accusing her of sometimes taking an unfair cut of their sex earnings and charging prostitutes rent of $1,500 a month to live in her brothel home. "She watches me, she took down the blinds before I moved in," said one worker. Another said, "She was very cold . . . just a time bomb."

In 2008 a production crew, developing a television series on failed beauty queens to be hosted by John Waters, was in Seattle filming interviews for a segment on Rose Marie. The willowy and shapely Madam Washington looked damn good at sixty-eight. She agreed to be interviewed for the series, she said, to set the record straight, claiming there was never any little black book with the names of her customers as stated (and sealed) in court records. She still seemed hurt that *Seattle Weekly* reported some of her customers parked at a neighborhood school. "They never did!" she protested.

She was proudly an ex-madam, recalling how she was asked to leave town whenever elections approached—apparently so as not to be linked to her whip-me, hurt-me politician customers—and said "close friends" on the police force often tipped her off when the vice squad was about to bust her massage and escort operations.

She didn't want to be asked about any names or specific details, something she reiterated in later phone calls. She said she had given up both drinking and the career that made her infamous. She took care of seven dogs and was a bit of a crusader for sobriety. Once she had pleaded guilty in 2000, she said, "there was no way to continue on—other than move to Nevada, I suppose."

As of this writing, the beauty queen series has yet to air; however, her distant neighbor Frank was about to get a lot of exposure.

FAMILY VALUES

The Rising Son

"We've always been very close. He's always given me advice on
everything. He gives me advice on what shoes to wear."

Frank Colacurcio did his time in Texas and made freedom by
1986. To the shock and awe of no one, he was almost immediately charged with a parole violation for assaulting a waitress
at his Sugar's club in Shoreline—grabbing her, kissing her, and
offering her $100 for sex.

He "spoke to me about going over to his house and having a good time for a few hours, but I thought he was joking
because he was married," the dancer told police. "He told me I
could go home with him and make an easy one. He told me he
meant $100." Then, according to the eighteen-year-old, dirty
old Frank grabbed "the lapels of my coat and pulled me toward
him. He kissed me, sticking his tongue into my mouth." She
quit the next day.

A district court judge gave Frank a wrist tap and did not
feel he was in violation of his parole. And hell, he *was* old. As
well, his mother, Christina, had just died at age ninety-one. In
addition to her own brood of kids, she left behind twenty-nine

165

grandchildren, thirty-four great-grandchildren, and two great-great-grandchildren. It might have been a sobering moment for Frank, whose father had died nineteen years earlier. He seemed to dip below the police horizon for awhile. Maybe he realized that prison was no respite for a guy hitting his seventies. But in three years he was headed back.

At seventy-three, Frank and his rising partner in crime, son Frankie, twenty-eight, were accused of skimming from their two topless clubs in Anchorage, the Good Times and the Wild Cherry. This had gone on for most of ten years—Frankie did the bookkeeping while dad was in stir. Their old pal, ex-con Gil Pauole, to whom they had loaned $200,000 to start up the clubs, had skimmed as much as $60,000 per month in profits at the direction of Frank and Frankie. In 1990 the two were charged with federal tax violations. Frank must have had it marked on his calendar of upcoming events: every ten years, get indicted.

But unlike in 1984, when Pauole was a reluctant witness at Frank's tax trial, this time the ex-employee was ready to tell all about father and son and their "ins-and-outs" accounting system. The government, after Pauole got involved in an Alaska contract killing, turned him into a federal informant.

During his time in Anchorage, Pauole had hooked up with a local attorney, Neil Mackay, who was looking for a contract killer, Pauole claimed. It wasn't the first time, apparently, Mackay had sought out a hit man: the attorney's wife had died in a car bombing allegedly engineered by Mackay, though that was never proven. Now he was involved in a nasty child-custody battle with his brother-in-law, Alaska Airlines pilot Bob Pfeil.

Pauole, familiar with the caverns of Anchorage's underworld, said he hired a hit man who shot Pfeil to death in 1985. Not long after, the killer was busted along with Pauole and Mackay, who was tried twice but never convicted. Facing at least twenty years in prison, Pauole turned government informant, testifying against Mackay and the killer. Pauole also supplied the feds with inside financial information about Frank and several of his brothers, who ran nude dance operations in Phoenix. He then disappeared into the witness protection rabbit hole.

Pauole appeared ready to testify against his "father" Frank, as he once called him, and against Frankie at their scheduled 1991 trial in Seattle. But it was cancelled. Frank and Frankie sized up their odds, took a deep breath, and pleaded guilty to tax evasion.

In consideration of Frank's perceived dotage, the court gave him two-and-a-half years behind bars, five years probation, and a $10,000 fine. "I struggled with this one," said Judge John Coughenour, explaining that he ultimately decided to be kind to the septuagenarian. He worried that after the earlier convictions, Frank still hadn't gotten the message. If he'd been any younger, it would have been "thirty years instead of thirty months," he said. Age was also a sentencing factor for a third person involved in the tax case. Nick Furfaro, Frank's old friend since they started up the Magic Inn on Union Street in the fifties, pleaded guilty to a misdemeanor and, as part of his short sentence, was told he had to give up his job running Sugar's in Shoreline. Furfaro asked the court for mercy: don't make him quit, he said, he's too old. He had a family to support, and there wasn't much call elsewhere for sixty-five-year-old nudie bar managers. The judge politely refused.

Frank leveraged his own age even further, convincing the judge he should be allowed to spend the summer fishing before reporting to a California federal prison in October. His attorneys had practically begged to let the old man return to the sea for what they called probably his last fishing trip ever.

Young Frankie got off even lighter: three years in prison, most of it suspended. Out in six months, he got married on New Year's Eve, 1991. Prison "didn't bug me that much, except you don't have women, which is horrible," he said. Terri, thirty, his new wife, was one of his club managers and had a daughter from an earlier marriage. They were happy, and Frankie's star was rising. His dad's recent conviction and the years in stir were sure to take their toll; Frank already had gained forehead and seemed to be permanently bent forward. The trimmer Frankie, though he sported prematurely gray cropped hair, was a hipper Frank with more appreciation for the rigors of prison. It seemed time he stepped up, even if his dad thought he was something of a cream puff and hadn't experienced the hard knocks Frank Sr. had. (Among Junior's prized possessions were a comic book collection and a statue of St. Francis dating back to his grade school days.) Frankie's mom wasn't particularly enamored of or confident about her son filling his dad's shoes. "I feel Frankie— if he had to run it [the business] and his father wasn't around," said Jackie Colacurcio, "I don't think he's capable of doing it."

With the steadying hand of his father's longtime partners, son Frankie began attempts to expand the business, picking up several club properties on the Eastside and in other suburban areas. But he almost immediately ran into neighborhood opposition and irate city councils and had to pull back. He and his partners refocused on the existing clubs, which had recently shed one of their major business impediments, the state Liquor Control Board. The clubs had stopped selling booze and began charging $5 for a one-drink-minimum soda pop. They no longer had to worry about excessive vomit in the men's room and liquor inspectors with their thick rule books. They would lose the considerable profit from drink sales, but the girls could make that up. The clubs told dancers they would have to start paying to dance, from $75 to more than $100 a shift, though they could keep any money they made from table dances or tips. The clubs knew they had a captive employment pool. Prospective dancers often arrived needy and vulnerable at the Talents West hiring offices in an old stand-alone building in Lake City. Bob Payton, the cordial personnel director—and house sitter when Frank was off doing time—said the young job seekers regularly told him, "I have no money, I'm broke, my boyfriend left me, my husband beat me, I'm on welfare, can I get paid under the table—things like that."

As Frankie edged closer to the helm, his new marriage had started to come apart. By 1993 the son had moved into his dad's Lake Forest Park home, and within a year he was talking divorce. "I was convinced our marriage was over and I was in another relationship," he admits. "Every time I tried to discuss divorce with Terri, she simply lost it."

Father Frank was back from prison by late 1993, more lines in his face, fighting off the sunlight with tinted bifocals, his hearing fading. And now his wife was on her way out, too, having filed divorce papers while he was in prison.

Jackie Colacurcio had visited Frank just one time while he was locked up before in California. This time she didn't want to see him even once, inside the walls or out. It was one thing to put up with some of his catting around and money games, but there's a breaking point and she'd passed it. A friend of hers says Jackie didn't like her son being involved in her husband's nudie business, and of course it had turned out as she had feared: Junior, who had been working around the clubs since the early eighties, was following Senior's footsteps not only through the business but into prison. ("We've always been very close," Frankie once said. "He's always given me advice on everything. He gives me advice on what shoes to wear.")

In divorce court, where the case dragged out over almost three years, Jackie asked for half of their community property. When Frank was released during the proceedings, she quickly sought a restraining order, saying she didn't want him in the house taking things or going through papers. As well, "I am concerned about my safety and well-being," she said. "I have suffered considerable stress during the last several years and the effect of the stress has been cumulative to the point where I would not be able to manage having [Frank] residing in the same residence." Her husband, she added, "has had a long history of business activities in connection with topless dancing clubs and like facilities. He has been imprisoned on several occasions for having not accurately accounted for his income and his activities generally. He just completed a prison term for failing to report his income to the Internal Revenue Service. He pleaded guilty on February 8, 1991, to felony counts of aiding and abetting in the preparation of false corporate tax returns for two topless nightclubs in Anchorage, Alaska. . . . [Frank] has been identified in local and national criminal proceedings as a head of a syndicate or a network of topless dance and like entertainment businesses in a number of states. He has served prison terms for income tax evasion and the transportation of gambling equipment. His record extends back as far as the 1960s to the best of my knowledge and he has been identified as being associated with organized crime and gambling syndicates before the Senate Rackets Committee. . . . He has concealed any interest he has in these businesses and has largely avoided having assets held in his name. The federal government was compelled to establish his unreported income on the basis of his net worth."

Frank enjoyed a lavish lifestyle, Jackie added, and had large sums of cash available to him. But, as the government investigations indicated, finding his money and assets was never an easy task. With a restraining order, Jackie said, maybe she could keep him from hiding more of them.

Ultimately Frank, seventy-seven, and Jackie, fifty-four, divided up almost $2 million in land, assets, household goods, and jewelry, including Frank's $110,000 worth of baubles, watches, medallions, and a coin collection. In the 1994 settlement, she got a Lincoln, a $350,000 house in Kitsap County, stocks, and other property. He got to keep his Rolex, the home at Sheridan Beach, and two other properties worth $400,000. Frank also got a reprimand from his ex's lawyers for being less than truthful. "Clearly," said the attorney, "the respondent [Frank] did not make a forthright and candid disclosure of his assets and financial affairs. . . . This case represented a difficult problem of proof because of the respondent's background."

Requirements of his five-year-long parole prevented Frank from getting back into the topless business. But not long after leaving prison, he began showing up now and then at the Talents West agency, which displayed some of his infamous press clips on the wall. The office also featured an exceptionally large, handsome desk at which Frank sometimes sat proudly. He looked like the president of the United States or something, said a former employee. Frank's gray hair was thinning, he was gaining jowly age lines, and his doctor, Frank Gleeson, determined Frank was experiencing polycythemia rubra vera, a condition that can lead to thrombophlebitis, or blood clotting.

Obviously, that last prison stretch wasn't good for his health. Yet, within a year, he was headed back. Those infrequent Talents West drop-ins turned into a regular gig, and he had begun interviewing job applicants—then feeling them up. Unable to control that aging libido, Frank one afternoon grabbed, kissed, fondled, and propositioned a teenager he was interviewing for a dance job. The eighteen-year-old, who was also pregnant, said that Frank first asked her to "go home and cuddle and be lovey," then kissed her and offered her $500. As a preggie teen, she may not have been the great desire of Frank's heavy-breathing customers, but he thought she was hot.

"I freaked out," she said. "I mean, this is the scariest thing that's ever happened to me." She needed a job because, after getting pregnant, she'd dropped out of high school and then her boyfriend left her. When she walked into Talents West, Frank said he'd hire her immediately.

Prosecutors termed it indecent liberties, a violation of his probation, which prohibited involvement in the dance business and reappearances at the office. In a 1995 federal court session, Judge Coughenour looked down and, in terms of sentencing, saw a much younger Frank this time. He was no longer too old to lock up. "I told Mr. Colacurcio rather pointedly three-and-a-half years ago that I wanted him out of this business," said the judge, who then handed down a three-year term. At seventy-eight, Frank became a senior citizen of the Bastrop, Texas, federal pen.

Frankie, meanwhile, had told wife Terri they were going to be divorced, period. In response, Terri, like Frank's wife, asked for a restraining order "because my husband has a terrible temper and I am concerned about his reaction to this [divorce] motion. He has threatened violence although I know of no specific acts of violence. He has also been living away from this home since separation and I no longer want him in this house." Frankie was paying her $6,000 a month to live on, and he was earning about $680,000 a year, she said.

In rebuttal, Frankie thought it was Terri who was out of control. As he explained in a court deposition:

"The businesses in which I am involved are focused on adult entertainment. The various entities either operate clubs or own the property on which the clubs are located. Most of these interests predate our marriage substantially. The businesses are under constant attack from local regulatory agencies [like the cops and FBI]. The primary draw in the clubs is table dancing and recent enactments of what is known in the industry as the 'four foot rule' have substantially compromised the profitability of these ventures. Most recently the Washington Supreme Court upheld these ordinances." (Over the years, the Colacurcios spent heavily on legal and lobbying efforts to maintain the "intimacy" of their clubs, and the sex parlors they called the VIP rooms. Their biggest threat wasn't police, but the four-foot separation rule. A no-groping zone between dancer and customer would mean "financial devastation," the Colacurcios said in court. Though some suburban cities drove nude dancing out of town with such a rule, Frank and Frankie prevailed in other communities and went all in to head off a proposed separation rule in Seattle in 2006, teaming politically with their competitor, Déjà Vu dance-chain operator Roger Forbes. Together, the two rivals donated more than $850,000 to defeat the planned no-feely-zone law.)

"Terri was very familiar with this type of business," Frankie went on. "She managed two of the clubs in which I am involved in 1985 and 1986 (that's when I met her) and prior to that had managed a club in Texas. She considered these ventures my businesses and recognized the very significant risk in their continued operation." And while Terri would get monthly support and substantial assets—a house in Snohomish County, three cars, and a motor home (Frankie got three cars and a flatbed trailer)—she was upset about the apparent loss of her daughter's affections. Frankie had officially adopted the girl during the marriage, and now she wanted to go stay at Frankie's place. "Terri," he said, "has been extremely volatile . . . [she] called the house, woke me up and demand that I put [the girl] on the

phone. . . . The conversation was obviously distressing. . . . "
Later, Terri brought over the girl's pets and left them in a box
on Frankie's porch. "I went to the house and found the ani-
mals in boxes with minimal air holes in the hot sun on the hot
asphalt driveway." He got them to the vet in time, he said.

Within two years, while his dad was in prison at Bastrop for
the probation violation, Frankie had a new gal named Teena.
They flew off to Las Vegas in 1999 and got married. It shaped
up like a successful relationship this time. They had a million-
dollar home on the other side of Lake Washington in Kirkland,
and Teena gave birth to three children.

With old Frank off learning his lesson again, father and son
seemed on a road less crooked and fell from the headlines.

Not that there was any shortage of memorable Seattle vice
figures to take up the slack.

Bookies and Gamers

"I realize that Cliff has again broken the law. I realize that
this probably won't be the last time unless every sport,
including turtle racing, is outlawed."

N ghia Dung Luu liked to tell strangers he sewed garments in
Tukwila. And apparently did quite well at it. So well, in fact,
that his associates and federal agents bestowed the title of "Ong
Chu" on him, Vietnamese for "Mr. Boss." He earned it not for
his success with the sewing machine, but his day spent on the
telephone. In 1999 he became what the feds said was Seattle's
all-time bookmaking kingpin, running a $300,000-a-month col-
lege and professional sports betting operation out of the phone
rooms at his Bellevue home and his brother-in-law's apartment
in Renton.

The short, slight forty-nine-year-old immigrated to the
United States and Seattle in the eighties. Within a decade he
was a great success at taking, and winning, bets. He amassed
more than $2 million in property bought with his profits—all
of which he signed over to the government in a plea bargain.
It included the house in Bellevue, some of its furniture, and

most of its home entertainment electronics; a nineteen-unit apartment building in Seattle's Rainier Valley; two cars and a pickup truck; $138,310 in cash, $231,045 in stock accounts, and $7,301 in bank accounts; and two dozen gold and diamond jewelry items, including three eye-candy bracelets: one with 27 diamonds, another with 147 diamonds, and a third with 159 diamonds.

Ong Chu had been on the cops' radar since the early nineties, when he was already flush—worth perhaps $1 million, but, as part of his cover, living in subsidized housing. He was arrested several times early on—once after vice cops placed at least $18,000 in undercover bets and lost most of it—but he was not prosecuted at the time. Though a bust is usually enough of a hint to find another line of work, the confident boss went on booking and talking: an FBI wiretap in 1998 picked up 974 calls in nine days. Translators listened to Luu take his agents' action and argue in Vietnamese over money: "You owe $10,920. You don't rip me off!"

No one is certain how much the operation won, paid out, or earned in vigorish—the cost, usually 10 percent, a bookie charges for taking bets. But, by another measure of his wealth, Ong Chu seemed as successful as a Microsoft manager: his personal tax return for 1997 showed $36.2 million in stock trades—buying and selling at a rate of $3 million a month.

Other Seattle bookies say they were impressed. But "he broke two rules," said Tommy Ryan, who had successfully dabbled in betting for almost twenty-five years. "Never get greedy, and never think they're not after you."

Cliff Winkler Jr., who was one of Ong Chu's predecessors, seconded that. "They" were always after Winkler, and getting caught had left him with a $1 million IRS tab, he said. He also endured enough stress to require open-heart surgery in the eighties.

Winkler, unlike Ong Chu, was more of a traditionalist and considered bookmaking an irresistible art form. He worked the phone hard between jaunts to pay winners and hunt down losers, and tried not to be greedy about it. He banked thousands of dollars weekly by expertly balancing his books—handing off some bets to other bookies so the wagering didn't weigh too heavily on the outcome of just one game. A balanced book that pays off winners and losers equally guarantees the bookmaker a profit from the vigorish.

"I'm sure," said Winkler's attorney Murray Guterson after his client was hauled before a federal judge in Seattle, "if Damon Runyon were telling you about Cliff Winkler, he would assure you that, just like Sky Masterson in *Guys and Dolls*, his marker is always good. No less than Benny Southstreet or Nicely-Nicely Johnson should Cliff Winkler be a part of the Broadway of the 1930s." Federal prosecutor Ron Neubauer thought Winkler was incorrigible, though he seemed to say so with grudging admiration. "I realize that Cliff has again broken the law. I realize that this probably won't be the last time unless every sport, including turtle racing, is outlawed."

The bookmaking approaches used by Winkler and Ong Chu have been replaced by progress—in particular, online betting. It is done both legally and illegally, and attracts millions with a computer and credit card. With fewer traditional practitioners, though, that likely leaves the old-timers' records forever intact.

That could be said as well for a onetime bartender at the exclusive Harbor Club in downtown Seattle who may have won, in absentia, Seattle's biggest illegal bet ever.

A club member says it went down thusly:

In the late eighties, the private dining and social club initiated a betting board for a Super Bowl game, offering squares to members for $1,000 each. Like the legal one-hundred-square dollar boards you see in bars, the winner is determined by matching two numbers to team scores at the end of each quarter. But this board was considerably different. For high rollers only, it would pay $25,000 a quarter—$100,000 overall.

The day before the game, all the squares were filled in, the numbers drawn, and the money and the board then seemingly locked away. The bartender turned off the lights and went home.

After, that is, he opened the safe and took the $100,000 with him.

The club was closed on Super Bowl day. But the winners—three of them, one winning two quarters—showed up the next day to collect.

No money. No bartender. No answer at his home.

He was gone, never to be found.

Police said they'd heard this story but never bothered to try to confirm it. For one thing, no one had lodged an official complaint.

"What can they say?" a vice detective asked. "'This guy has $100,000 that we bet illegally? Arrest him so you can take us to jail?'"

In his book, said the cop, "It was the perfect crime."

That's something another career criminal named Smooth is never likely to hear.

Cracking a Vice Record

"Like many of these guys when they're young, he couldn't
figure out how to market himself, and found the best
thing he could market was drugs."

In the annals of Seattle vice, there's been nobody quite like
Stacy Earl Stith, street name Smooth. Police figured they'd
encountered him as many as two hundred times over his three-
decade drug career. Of course it never took great law enforcing to
snare him. In the nineties, when a prostitute at Seventh and Bell
asked what he was doing, Smooth said, "Selling, man!"—and
pulled a cache of rocks from his pants pocket. "I sell to everyone!"
The undercover police hooker beckoned her backup team, and
Smooth went to jail. A decade later, plainclothes cops were nab-
bing another dealer when Smooth and his girlfriend made two
drug sales practically in front of them in City Hall Park, next to
the King County Courthouse, where he'd already been convicted
of nine felonies. He was arrested and went to jail only hours after
he had been released from prison that same day.

Smooth was mostly a street dealer, a cop's easy quota. He
distributed his stones, as he calls crack cocaine, hand to hand

from Belltown to SoDo or by vehicle to home-delivery customers in the burbs. At times he stowed the tiny bags of stones in his car's or van's engine compartment, from where the bags would occasionally drop onto the street, requiring Smooth to hop out and run back through traffic to retrieve them. Other times he'd spread the stash around, such as the day he was found with fifteen grams of marijuana separated into sixteen different bags in his pants pocket, twenty-seven grams of marijuana and nine grams of crack in the trunk of his vehicle, eleven grams of crack in bags tucked into his waistband, and forty-nine grams of bagged crack in his, well, crack—his underwear.

An NFL-size black man in his late thirties, his braided hair often dangling from under a sideways ball cap, Smooth has been relentlessly, if ineptly, selling and using drugs in Seattle since the eighties. Along the way he's compiled a criminal record that's something of a record itself, authorities say: adding up misdemeanors and felonies since the mideighties, he has 112 convictions. Not arrests, *convictions*: ninety-four misdemeanors and eighteen felonies, revolving through the doors of juvenile court to municipal court to district court to superior court to federal court, from traffic and theft offenses and weapons and assault charges to burglary and crack sales. His first day in court was at age thirteen; his most recent, in January 2009, at age thirty-nine.

By most accounts, he is the most persistent nonmurderous criminal in Seattle history, the vice record holder in the field of drug violations. "I have never seen anyone with this number of convictions around here," says King County deputy prosecutor Andy Colasurdo. He couldn't think of another violator who even came close. Some had a similar number of felonies, but "most of them only had twenty to forty misdemeanors."

For all those convictions, Smooth has served an aggregate fourteen years behind bars in local jails and state prisons, by Colasurdo's count. He had been sentenced to considerably more time, but his terms typically ran concurrently and he was usually released early. So he's had to work fast, scoring those 112 convictions in just eleven years of freedom. That's an average of ten guilty verdicts per year.

"He," by the way, could mean Stacy Stith or James Howard or Cal Beaver or Eric Smith, among others. Smooth has used eighteen aliases, five dates of birth, and four Social Security numbers. It's possible, given that older court documents are often incomplete and crimes could be recorded under some of those aliases, Smooth's record may be even longer.

On the street, beat cops would recognize him on sight and assume he was in violation of something—parole, work release, curfew, loitering—most likely there was an arrest warrant somewhere with his name on it. (Court records show he had been sought on fifty-two warrants over two decades for a variety of crimes and failures to appear in court.)

Smooth was a sometimes hapless lawbreaker. One early morning call brought officers to a smashed display window at the downtown Bon Marché, where they found him standing nearby with a pile of stolen clothes at his feet, department store tags flapping in the wind. But he was no comic figure. He sped away from one police stop and careened around Central District corners in his '85 Buick. The chase ended when he slid sideways to a stop, tossed a loaded 40-caliber Glock out a window, and bailed. An officer pinned him down but needed backup help to get him into handcuffs. Smooth was later convicted of being an armed felon. He also has six convictions for resisting or obstructing police officers. Once, holding $1,300 in powder and rock cocaine, Smooth had to be Tasered four times before two cops could cuff him. Court records describe him as "a high-risk offender who presents a significant threat to the community."

Smooth has been found guilty so often that the word may be meaningless to him. Once he reached fifty convictions—as he did while still in his teens—what was another fifty? Colasurdo, who also worked as a special assistant prosecutor for the U.S. attorney's office, thought Smooth was either incapable of changing his criminal ways or unwilling to do so. To his Seattle attorney John Crowley, though, "He has a dope problem. Like many of these guys when they're young, he couldn't figure out how to market himself, and found the best thing he could market was drugs." Smooth was five days shy of his thirteenth birthday when he was first arrested, for third-degree theft. He was convicted a week later in King County juvenile court, but given no time, then convicted of theft fifteen more times in the following three years, with sentences ranging from a few days to a few months. He later informed a drug counselor that he had begun using marijuana at age twelve and continued to smoke it through adulthood. He started drinking as a juvenile, and as an adult could down a fifth of liquor daily. Smooth first used cocaine at sixteen, a habit that grew to more than ten rocks a day, he said.

Smooth has told counselors, attorneys, and judges that he just can't beat his addiction, and that's what led to his life of crime, which includes convictions for felony theft, forgery, and burglary. Court records show he's done time in juvenile hall for possession of marijuana and cocaine, and has eleven felony convictions for possession or distribution of crack cocaine, not counting two charges that were dropped. When a Seattle cop stopped him for erratic driving and displaying license plates that had expired four years earlier, he was found to also be driving without a license, something he'd already been convicted of twenty times. He was worried the cop might see the bag of rocks on his floorboard, so he confessed to having just smoked weed. Really, he said, "If I had stones, I would have run or something." The cop found the drugs anyway.

Born in St. Louis and raised in the Seattle area, Smooth dropped out of high school as a teen. His mother and father divorced when he was young. His mom remarried and ran a day care. Family members couldn't be reached, but prosecutor Colasurdo says Smooth "had parents at home who loved him, provided for him, and served as good role models." He worked at times in the construction industry, but court records state his drug use had a "negative impact on his employment . . . such as being late for work, diminished productivity, absences, and using [drugs] at work, and termination."

For much of his adult life, when not in jail, prison, or a halfway house, Smooth rented apartments or was homeless. He suffered a minor heart attack from cocaine use, he told a drug counselor, who noted in his report that Smooth "enjoys playing basketball, fishing, and dancing with his girlfriend," who was also busted for drugs. He married a Tacoma woman in 1998. Court papers showed they have a child and that she filed for divorce in 2004. It did not seem a happy union. Smooth, she said in her filing, "resided in the penitentiary for the duration of the marriage." He was out for a while in 2004. That September—the month he and his wife officially separated—Smooth was arrested for possession of crack and marijuana, and was booked and released. Twelve days later he was arrested for selling crack and again was booked and released. Less than a month later he was arrested again for possession. He awaited trial in jail and in 2005 was convicted of all three charges. He faced a maximum of 120 months, but got just twenty-four, and ultimately did just twelve. On the day he was released, he was arrested after officers observed him selling drugs in City Hall Park. After being booked and released, he was arrested eleven days later after being found in possession of crack and marijuana.

"I've been to prison several times," he told one of his drug counselors in a note, and had received some treatment, as well as gone cold turkey to kick his habit. "I always come home and use drugs and alcohol. I've been a drug addict for 25 years. Please, for once, can you give me a chance to get sober and stay clean by going through with the recommendation [for drug counseling]? Thank you." He was allowed to enroll as an outpatient at a treatment center and after completing about a third of an eighteen-month program, he bailed.

Then came a phone call from a drug customer named Jersey, wanting to buy some crack.

"I've been charging $750," Smooth told Jersey. "You know, I just give you a deal . . . my prices [between] me and you don't be the same prices to everybody else. I've been getting $250 a quarter [ounce]. Two a quarter, you know." Jersey agreed to meet up. He then handed the phone back to a Seattle vice detective. Jersey was his informant.

Smooth met with Jersey at a First Hill parking lot and sold him an ounce of crack for $700. Seattle police detectives watched and took pictures. The following month, outside a convenience store in Tukwila, Smooth sold Jersey another ounce, also under surveillance. A week later, after another buy was set up, plainclothes cops moved in on Smooth's Dodge Caravan at a Denny's parking lot in Tukwila. They found eleven ounces of crack and three ounces of powder cocaine hidden in the engine compartment. Another quarter-ounce rock was discovered under the gas cap. Police began typing up four charges—two for possession and two for distribution of cocaine—potentially his 109th through 112th convictions.

Under federal law, as a career offender, Smooth could be prosecuted not only for his recent offenses, but, in a sense, for all of them. And he easily passed the test—a convicted federal offender needs only two prior felonies to receive an enhanced sentence as a career criminal. He also reoffended every time he was released, Colasurdo observed, and "Not once did he repay the mercy shown to him by the prosecutors or the courts with law-abiding behavior." Prosecutors sought thirty years in federal prison. If Smooth was convicted and survived incarceration, he would be almost seventy upon release.

The feds offered Smooth a plea deal, but he chose to go to trial, claiming the informant, whom he met in his drug-counseling classes, talked him into getting back into drugs before entrapping him into selling again. The June 2008 trial lasted three days, swiftly followed by a guilty verdict. In 2009 U.S. District Court Judge James L. Robart sentenced Smooth on his 112th conviction to federal prison for twenty-four years, with ten years supervised release if and when he gets out. Counting time for good behavior Smooth could earn while locked up, the Federal Bureau of Prisons projects his release date to be July 30, 2028, a month before his fifty-ninth birthday.

"Damn, it hurts to watch," said Crowley, his attorney. "There's a little boy in every one of these guys I represent."

That's something Seth Warshavsky might say too. He's not an attorney, but he had to hire a lot of them.

Porn.com

"The Pope and I share many of the same interests."

By the turn of the twenty-first century, Frank Colacurcio's downsized nudie dancing empire faced stiff opposition from a growing phenom called the Internet—and in particular from someone who grew up in Microsoft's neighborhood, near Frank's old "ghost farm." Young computer geek Seth Warshavsky came out of suburban Bellevue and quickly levitated to multimillion-dollar success as Seattle's and one of America's foremost online pornographers. Depending on who was characterizing him, he was either a genius, a misogynist, a respected global businessman, an exploiter of children, the Bill Gates of porn, or the Larry Flynt of cyberspace. He was one of the few Web entrepreneurs of any kind to turn a profit. Or so it seemed.

In his early twenties, he had already been sued by the Pope and Pamela Anderson Lee, caused a riled-up competitor to spit in his face, and was arrested for choking his former girlfriend during a limo ride in Las Vegas (he claimed he was trying to keep her from jumping out). He was promising to take his fast-rising adult-entertainment company public and had even appeared before Congress to discuss online sex (he was for it). His eclectic mix of Web sites offered casino betting, psychic advice, housing loans, and sex-change operations—such as turning a male Florida government worker into a woman named Julie by removing his/her penis.

Warshavsky was gearing up to sell art and music over the Net and awaiting the arrival of higher-speed, TV-quality video on the home computer to transmit picture-perfect sex live from Seattle. His intent was to surpass the lower-quality sex acts he was already transmitting from his Pioneer Square studio—"free" to paid members—supposedly a hundred thousand of them paying $25 a month or $175 a year. Amid a jumble of beds, stages, showers, and video cameras, men and women earned all of $20 an hour in the converted warehouse performing what began as strip dancing in 1996 and evolved into live sex: alone, with objects, or with each other. On the loft's stages, thirty-five technicians, directors, and young performers would become locked in dramatic productions of masturbation and intercourse—simulated in the sense that there was no apparent ejaculation or penetration. Many of the performers—some of them onetime local nude club dancers and their boyfriends—undressed and rolled about, semi–banging away for hours on end as directors in a booth guided the joysticks of remote cameras, part of what Warshavsky claimed was $3 million worth of push-video and state-of-the-art graphics systems.

Warshavsky claimed his revenues topped $50 million a year, and he was planning to take his company, Internet Entertainment Group, public with a forthcoming stock offering. He tried to dress things up a bit, calling himself an "adult content provider" rather than "porn king" or "smut merchant." That was also why he, for the moment, was keeping his live sex mostly soft-core. "We're pretty conservative when it comes to explicitness," he said.

Masturbation, on the other hand, along with another by-product, publicity, were his specialties. Warshavsky said he personally didn't spank the monkey, what with all these women available to him, but he certainly hoped his customers did. He instead relentlessly pounded the publicity-mongering machinery, scoring PR points while occasionally sounding like a tin-horn Hugh Hefner. He delighted in picking on Hollywood targets sure to gain him some ink, such as Pamela Anderson Lee and then-estranged hubby, Tommy Lee. He staved off all their court attempts to stop his site from showing and selling their infamous honeymoon sex video. He similarly battled Poison singer Bret Michaels, whose video of *him* and Anderson having sex was on Warshavsky's future playlist. Radio shrink Dr. Laura Schlessinger likewise failed in her attempt to force the removal of a dozen embarrassing naked still photos taken two decades earlier (and sold for $50,000 to Warshavsky) by her ex-lover. Actor Kelsey Grammer filed a lawsuit when he thought Warshavsky had possession of a homemade video of the one-time *Frasier* star making love, but four days later dropped the suit "like a red-hot crack pipe," said a gleeful Warshavsky, in reference to Grammer's admitted drug use.

Warshavsky also offered any member of Congress a discount at a whorehouse in Nevada. It was done so in gratitude, he said, after being called before a congressional hearing in 1999 to testify on proposed Internet adult-content regulations. He suggested creation of a secure zone in cyberspace with "dot.adult" addresses, figuring it could be blocked from children's access by a V-chip. Legislators seemed impressed, but it was also a sly business move by Warshavsky intended to keep critics at bay.

The Pope was his best score, however. Warshavsky linked his sex site to another that was covering Pope John Paul II's 2000 visit to St. Louis. To make sure Catholics were properly horrified, Warshavsky padded his site with accounts of papal sex scandals and dirty religious jokes. In a suit by the church that delighted Warshavsky no end, a federal judge in St. Louis ordered that he sever his link to the Pope coverage. "The Pope and I share many of the same interests," Warshavsky snickered in a publicity release. "Sex is what drives our business and sex is a main concern of the Pope."

What drove Warshavsky to appoint himself as America's dirty-sex laureate? He was a Bellevue High dropout who later got his GED off campus, he recalled in his nasally monotone, offering a vaguely toothy smile. Short and spare, he looked the mischievous kid sitting behind his oversize desk in a skyscraper near Pike Place Market—except that this kid turned his first million before he turned twenty-one. By nineteen—the same age as Bill Gates when he began to assemble Microsoft—Warshavsky discovered the easy money available from phone sex. Borrowing $7,000, he and a partner launched 1-800-GET SOME. He hired frothy-voiced, but not necessarily attractive, women to talk men into a lather and, finally, a climax. The venture grew from crude beginnings to a worldwide operation that, Warshavsky said, grossed $60 million in just a few years. By age twenty-two, he saw the future and it was still phone sex, but with pictures. Pirating a streaming-video sex site idea from a Canadian online pioneer, he launched Candyland.com, his original online porn site, in January 1996, changing the name to Clublove.com after toy maker Hasbro sued for name infringement on its Candy Land board game. By 2000 his expanded operations netted $15 million annually, he claimed, earning him mostly bemused admiration. *Wired* magazine called him "the

Bob Guccione of the 1990s," comparing him with the some-times unctuous *Penthouse* publisher. The *Wall Street Journal* said he was a "scrubbed and apple-cheeked . . . seasoned Web pub-lisher." *Adweek* found him to be a "freckle-faced, clean-cut Gen-Xer who recently bought a boat and likes water-skiing, but says he is bored when not working." ABCNews.com quoted him as saying, "My mother's proud of me."

Missing from most Warshavsky profiles was any mention of what helped make Mrs. W's son rich—jerking off. Without that vast market of self-abuse, Warshavsky might have remained the clothing salesman he once was. His aggressive business tac-tics also ticked off competitors, among them Joseph Kahwaty of iBroadcast, a Seattle pornographic video-feed supplier. Warshavsky obtained a restraining order against Kahwaty after he allegedly spit in Warshavsky's face and challenged him to fight outside a Pioneer Square bar (Kahwaty posted details of the near-fisticuffs battle on the Internet, writing: "I spit in the little pussy's face . . ."). Warshavsky later sued Kahwaty for $1 million, claiming assault and defamation, then dropped the suit.

But lawsuits, it turned out, were perhaps the greatest by-product of Warshavsky's rise and fall in a short decade. He continued to get good national press. But in the courtrooms, another story was being told: a parade of creditors were after him to pay his bills; he wasn't making anything like the money he claimed to be earning; and his half-a-million-dollar First Avenue condo suddenly went up for a forced sale. There were more than a dozen lawsuits involving creditors, suppliers, and ex-employees, debts and bounced checks. Unico Properties of Seattle, for one, said his monthly office rent check for $5,000 not only bounced, but that Warshavsky would not respond to a demand to make it good, and Unico was awarded a default judgment. He paid it only after a bench warrant was issued for his arrest.

By 2002 he had bailed from Seattle, for almost-as-far-away-as-you-can-get Thailand. His luxury condo was publicly auctioned off after he defaulted on an $845,000 promissory note, and he had transferred what was left of his debt-ridden sex business to a California corporation that continued to operate the Web sites. Then it got bad. According to a court deposition, an Internet Entertainment Group official was unable to come up with company financial statements in a recent collection case "because all the documents had been subpoenaed by the federal grand jury." The official said that "Mr. Warshavsky was personally under criminal investigation."

It turned out that, rather than building a sex empire, Warshavsky was building debt, stiffing customers, and hiding from process servers. From tits out to tits up, he had assembled a debt estimated at half a million dollars. He battled creditors for years thereafter with the help of his attorney, Gil Levy—who, coincidentally, happened to be the longtime attorney for Frank Colacurcio.

At almost the same time Warshavsky left town, Frank and Levy had become embroiled in the kind of legal problems that make Thailand such an enticing retreat.

CIVIC ORGASMS

Strippergate

"Gabrielle on the main stage. Black sparkling string bikini. She touched her anus, buttocks, massaged her breasts."

Political donations from Frank Colacurcio Jr. to Seattle City Council member Heidi Wills began to arrive one day in 2003, quietly kicking off a five-year political and vice scandal that, despite its relatively tame corruption, was the beginning of the likely end for father Frank. First to mention the donations was *Seattle Times* columnist Jean Godden, who wrote an April column item on Wills pointing out, "The councilwoman has already amassed a campaign chest large enough to scare most challengers away, although there are some anomalies in her contributors' list. Along with such establishment figures as developer Martin Selig and attorney Judith Runstad, Wills has received maximum contributions ($650 each) from Frank Colacurcio Jr. and his spouse, Teena Colacurcio. Frank Jr. and his father, Frank Colacurcio, have long been known as the kingpins of nude dancing." Godden, unknowingly then, was writing the first draft of a scandal that would lead to the downfall of Wills as well as Council member Judy Nicastro, thirty-eight, and the election of Godden, seventy-one, to Nicastro's Council seat just months later. With a campaign that included a promise of ethical reform in the wake of the Colacurcio donations to Nicastro, Godden beat five rivals in the September primary and then ousted incumbent Nicastro in November by six thousand votes.

In June that year, reporter James Bush of the *Seattle Sun* raised another question about the contributions, noting that Colacurcio had been lobbying the council for several years for a rezoning to expand parking at Rick's in Lake City. "Jaws dropped," he wrote, "when Seattle City Council member Wills unexpectedly joined the three members of the Council's Land Use Committee during an April 15 hearing.

> A few minutes later, Wills and Committee Chair Judy Nicastro voted to support the petition of Rick's, a Lake City Way topless club, to rezone a piece of single-family zoned land for use as a parking lot.
>
> Committee members Richard Conlin and Margaret Pageler voted against the application, which will be sent on to the full council with a divided report. Had Wills not shown up, the matter would still have gone forward, but with a "Do Not Pass" recommendation.
>
> So what's the deal? Has young feminist Wills morphed into a strip club booster? And are the club's owners seeking to "systematically pay off our City Council" through campaign contributions, as charged by one neighborhood activist.
>
> No and definitely not, responds Wills. She insists her vote to support the rezone is a tactical effort to improve behavior in the club's sometimes-rowdy parking lot. . . .

A July report in *Seattle Weekly* took the story another step forward, revealing that at least $38,000 in donations from the Colacurcio clan as well as rival strip club operator Roger Forbes had been doled out to the campaigns of Nicastro, Wills, and Jim

Compton. The *Times* and then the *P-I* followed with stories, as the Seattle Ethics and Elections Commission began a probe.

Soon the dependable Al Rosellini showed up. In several stories, the *Weekly* revealed that the former governor, along with Frank's other longtime attorney, Gil Levy, lobbied City Council members about the rezone. Rosellini also hosted fund-raisers and solicited campaign donations for the Council members. Big Al said there wasn't a problem with his rainmaking role; "it's just the political thing" you do come campaign time.

It turned out, as well, that the former governor owned a car wash on Lake City Way, which just happened to be next door to Rick's. Rosellini said he didn't know that Frank operated the nudie joint next door, but it wasn't something he'd likely know about at his age, ninety-three. He did learn about it later, he said, and some of Frank's overflow parking was using space at the Bigfoot Car Wash at night.

Rick's opened on its site in 1988, during one of Frank's respites from prison. Starting in 1989, the club sought rezoning of a small parcel of land abutting the site for use as parking. (While Rick's had forty-six spaces, plenty of parking to satisfy legal requirements, there were so many customers that all the cars couldn't fit into the lot at the busiest times.) Both in 1989 and 1998, the city turned down Rick's rezone application.

Neighbors had long opposed the rezone because of the sex that went on in the parking lot, they said. Frank wasn't too subtle about what he was selling, they said, pointing to his Web site, SeattleTopless.com, where viewers were offered hard-core porn, animated screwing, and, next to a woman's photo, the chance to "cum take a ride on this slippery slut." Police in plainclothes regularly showed up for the action too. Their mission was to while away the afternoons watching the girls undress and grope, and record it all on audiotape. "Gabrielle on the main

stage," one undercover cop said covertly into his minirecorder.
"Black sparkling string bikini. She touched her anus, buttocks,
massaged her breasts. Gabrielle has long brown hair, slightly on
the heavy side. Silver is on the main stage. She is wearing white
T-bar panties, white silky top. She has short blond hair and a
tattoo on her left upper arm and one on her left calf. She just
massaged her breasts, pinched her nipples, and is now massag-
ing her vagina." He endured the scene for an hour, then left a
tip from taxpayers.

The city notified Rosellini that he had violated zoning laws
by allowing patrons from Rick's to park on his car wash property.
Neighbors had reported the car wash was used for valet parking
at Rick's. Rosellini said he did not track the day-to-day affairs at
the car wash, leaving that to an on-site manager. Clearly, however, he felt piqued by the city's action. "I have title to this property," he said definitely. "There is a shortage of parking on Lake
City Way." He also felt solidarity with Rick's owner over the
parking issue. "We had the same problem," he observes.

In a written statement to the *Weekly*, Rosellini said that
"Recently, Gil Levy, attorney for Rick's, came to me to ask my
advice" on the club's parking lot problems. "I told them they
needed to do what any other business or citizen should do:
become politically active. Present your case. Use the political
process. As part of this effort, I volunteered to host a couple of
fund-raising events, as I have for many candidates for sixty years
of my political involvement. I organized the events, and I solicited the donations. None of the City Council members were
involved" in arranging the events.

Yet in an earlier interview, Rosellini denied asking people
to contribute to campaigns. "I urge people to support a candidate. I give them some political advice but tell them it's
up to them. I never solicit any contributions for anyone."

Apparently he realized that was a provable lie. He was part of the effort led by Frankie to provide cash to family and friends that would be forwarded as individual donations to the three Council members, Nicastro, Wills, and Compton. People associated with Colacurcio Jr. through business, marriage, or birth contributed—according to the *Weekly*'s updated count—at least $39,000 to the trio that voted for the rezone sought by Frank.

Thus began a potboiler named Strippergate that would involve probes by the city's ethics commission, the county prosecutor, and the FBI. Under media and ethics commission pressure, the three Council members returned the donations— giving Frank and Frankie all their money back. More proof for the boss that corruption paid.

Then the tide began to turn. Months later, the council ended up reversing the rezone vote. "I believe," said Council member Peter Steinbrueck in a grave pronouncement just before the vote, "our precious covenant of trust with the public has been broken. We will take this vote today to rescind the Lake City rezone legislation and wipe the slate clean." Council member Wills never gave a full account of why she suddenly showed up at the Land Use Committee meeting to cast a vote in favor of the rezone—an unusual appearance, given that she was not even a member of the committee. She did say she was a student of the Rosellini school of backroom politicking and had been mentored by the ex-governor. Nicastro said he was her mentor as well. Compton, meanwhile, wasn't saying anything. Though he was a longtime TV journalist, including network reporting for NBC, he avoided the press and carped at them when confronted. As *Weekly* reporter George Howland Jr. wrote: "It seems unfathomable, given his many years as a reporter, that he was ignorant of the unseemly nature of lobbying and donations from a family so tied to the rampant political corruption in Seattle's history. Yet he refuses to offer real information on how he committed such a grievous lapse in judgment."

Frankie, of all people, started talking. He called himself an "investor" and said his own contributions reflected an investment in good political candidates. It didn't pay off all that well, however. Both Nicastro and Wills lost their reelection bids, and Compton, though reelected to the council, subsequently decided to retire. Strippergate also may have struck home, literally, for Frankie. He and wife Teena, who had helped him contribute some of the City Council money, were divorcing, and she was taking the house. Unlike in Frankie's first divorce case, the depositions and most financial statements from this split were sealed at his request by the court, with no explanation given. It cannot even be determined which party sought the divorce.

But Teena did get the couple's $995,000 Kirkland home, property records show. And one of the few court documents mentioning money states that Frankie agreed to pay $9,000 in monthly child support for the three kids.

As for Frank, Strippergate ticked him off. The family name, it seemed to him, had once again been dragged through mob mud for no good reason. It was that Bobby Kennedy thing again. "The Mafia, all that talk, it's a farce," he told the *P-I*. "The opinions of my family and me, let's look where all that started: Someone who had nothing invented something and made lies."

Leave him alone, he said. He was just a regular businessman trying to make a living off naked women.

Man Among Boobs

"How does her ability to be truthful get affected by whether or not she danced in her underwear?"

S trippergate was far from over, however. An ethics commission review continued, and county prosecutor Norm Maleng was studying the campaign contributions for possible felony violations. Frank Colacurcio was also dealing with the death of his sister Frances Schmitz, sixty-eight, who was fatally burned in a natural gas explosion at her Bellevue home in September 2004—the gas company would eventually pay $8 million to Frances's family to settle a lawsuit over a corroded pipe. And Frank had a new criminal case on his hands. He'd been charged in municipal court with groping one of Rick's waitresses.

The waitress, Lauren Luttrell, twenty-three, claimed she was pressured by Rick's managers to dance in her underwear and had altogether refused demands to dance topless or nude, therein putting her waitressing job at risk. She was also sexually assaulted by a customer, she claims, but management took no corrective action. Then, on the day after New Year's 2004, she said, she was sexually propositioned and assaulted by old man Frank, who offered her money in exchange for sex. He also "grabbed her breast and rubbed her nipple" and had "on numerous occasions in the past sexually harassed female employees," she said.

The aging Frank—who wore a hearing aid for Luttrell's testimony—argued through his attorney that her claims were suspect because she was experienced in the field of sin. She had taken human sexuality courses in college and had, after all, danced in bra and panties. It was a sort of she-wanted-it defense. To that, Assistant City Attorney Derek Smith responded: "How does her ability to be truthful get affected by whether or not she danced in her underwear? It cannot be, any more than Tom Cruise could be impeached with his *Risky Business* dance if he was the victim of an assault." As for the college courses, Smith added, "So what? How does the existence of this fact make the assault less likely? Does it impeach the victim's credibility? Does it show that the victim is biased? Worked at a law firm in college? That the victim read the book *Disclosure* by Michael Crichton? How is that offer of proof relevant to the charge of assault?"

The name-dropping seemed to help: Frank was convicted of misdemeanor assault.

He quickly filed an appeal, and Luttrell then filed a civil suit in superior court, seeking damages from Frank and Frankie and their hiring agency, Talents West. Frank almost welcomed Luttrell's suit. The then-eighty-seven-year-old godfather of nude dancing maintained during the municipal court trial that the ex-waitress had set him up, pursuing criminal and human-rights complaints just so she could eventually lodge a civil lawsuit and seek damages. In part because that scenario was merely theoretical, the city court excluded some evidence and testimony that might have helped Frank defend himself. With the civil claim, Luttrell might have helped him make his case for a new criminal trial.

Frank's attorney Gil Levy, in an appeal of the city conviction, wrote in court papers that "the defense theory of the [criminal] case was that the complaining witness falsely accused Mr. Colacurcio of sexual assault in order to get money from him in a civil lawsuit." The trial court would not allow Frank to introduce such supporting evidence as his claim that Luttrell socialized with him and accepted monetary gifts and "never once" complained to managers about his conduct. Attorney Smith said that, throughout the criminal case, "Gil did argue that she was just doing this for the money a civil case would bring, and it didn't seem to have any impact on the jury's verdict. I don't see how the fact that she did file a civil case now changes anything."

The elderly stripper king—who likely never thought he'd live long enough to see a sexual harassment claim filed by a strip-club worker—received a stay in his sentence during the appeal. He was facing ninety days of home detention for the assault on Luttrell and—what is thought to pain Colacurcio the most—was banned from Rick's nudie club for two years. Levy said his client considered that penalty "draconian."

Frank quietly settled the lawsuit with Luttrell, however, and though he got a new assault trial, he was convicted again and given a lighter sentence, six months' probation. The city attorney agreed to the lesser term, he said, due to Frank's poor health.

Not that everyone thought he deserved mercy. Quietly moving along in the background then was a new federal investigation. Or maybe a continuation of the probe dating to the seventies, when the feds realized the best way to get Frank was to follow his money. Indeed, they were doing that. Investigators tailed Frank's associate and money-delivery man, Gil Conte, who was being paid $50,000 a year to oversee Sugar's and also drive to the clubs, pick up cash and receipts, then drive to the Talents West office, and later, to an apartment rented in his name about two miles away. Investigators set up video cameras to watch the apartment and tagged along on other occasions. As an investigator recounted:

> On July 20, 2004, Conte exited the apartment building carrying a medium-sized package. He placed the package in the trunk of his black 2001 Lincoln Town Car, bearing Washington State license plate 795-XPJ, and then reentered the apartment building. Approximately one minute later, Conte walked out of the building and drove away in the Town Car.

Frank may not have known, but surely suspected, he was being watched, as usual. Now and then, he dropped hints during phone calls recorded by the feds that "they" were likely out there trying to make a big crime out of a little sin. But by then, Frank had other things to worry about, and, with Frankie, another trial to go to.

Cornering the Vice Market

"If you give a hand job, charge for it. If you give a blow job, charge for it. If you don't charge for it, then you'll be fired."

Norm Maleng was elected King County prosecutor in 1978. But it wasn't until July 2005 that he first charged Frank Colacurcio with a felony. The seven-term prosecutor said he was of course familiar with the man who, for sixty-two years—dating back to when Maleng was three years old—had been striving to become Seattle's modest version of an organized criminal. But "No, never had the opportunity," Maleng said as he strolled down his office hallway in the King County Courthouse after a press conference. He had just charged Colacurcio and three others in the Strippergate case with nine criminal counts that included conspiracy. "It was always federal," Maleng said of Frank's legal troubles. "Remember, it was back in the fifties and sixties, I think, the early seventies, and it was federal, and if memory serves me, it was mostly income tax." This time, it was "political money laundering," in Maleng's words, the $39,000 that turned up in a two-year city and state investigation, secretly doled out by Colacurcio, his family, and his friends to the reelection campaigns of the three Seattle City Council members.

By then Frank had been to prison for criminal racketeering, tax skimming, probation violations, and of course the forties' carnal-knowledge conviction. One of Maleng's predecessors did the state prosecutorial honors then. After that, Colacurcio moved on to the big time, U.S. District Court, up the hill. Maleng says that Colacurcio's history did not play into the latest charges. "But," he said, stopping in the hallway, "everybody brings to the table what they have done, if you know what I mean."

With this sort of experience, the graying, stocky Frank knew when to pipe up or down. At his nice home with the pool at the north end of Lake Washington, he was answering a reporter's phone call but saying little about the charges. "Thing is, until this thing is over, I can't talk about it," said Frank, who was recovering from a minor surgery. Likewise mum was Frankie, who was charged in the conspiracy along with two of Frank's employees and friends, Gil Conte and office manager Marsha Furfaro, wife of Nick Furfaro, Frank's aging friend barred from running his club on Aurora Avenue. "Really, you have to talk to my attorney," Frank said pleasantly.

Maleng was confidant he had the evidence to convict Frank and friends, issuing nineteen pages of charges and supporting documents. They outlined an extensive probe into bank transactions and Frank's own business records, forming a long money trail. In legalese, the defendants were charged with conspiracy to offer a false instrument for filing or record, and knowingly procuring others to do the same. Tim Burgess, a former cop and one-time city ethics commissioner later elected to the City Council, called the Colacurcio business "a criminal enterprise that has been operating in our region for decades." Though the city's civil elections probe had hit a dead end, the prosecutor was able to bring criminal charges in large part by granting immunity to some of those involved, he said. That may have at least for the moment caused a stir in the Colacurcio family and divided the Furfaro family. Marsha Furfaro's daughters had told investigators they were reimbursed for their contributions by their mother, who of course worked out of Frank's Talents West office. Marsha Furfaro was already on record calling the funds a "bonus" from Frank and Frankie.

Once again, in on the picture—but almost out of focus, as usual—was ex-governor Al Rosellini. Despite his major rainmaking role in helping distribute Frank's money, he was not charged. "There is no evidence of any criminal wrongdoing" by Al, said Maleng. Others who may have donated political cash provided by Frank included John Rosellini, Al's son. Maleng wouldn't say what he thought Al Rosellini's real role was in Strippergate. It turned out that the ex-governor had passed out thousands in disguised Colacurcio funds and had witnessed—if not orchestrated—one of the cash handoffs, with Frank at his side. That exchange unfolded at the Emerald Queen, a onetime paddle-wheel boat turned into a floating casino by the Puyallup Tribe, anchored at the Port of Tacoma. Al and Frank were joined by a third man, longtime Tacoma civic and sports figure Stan Naccarato. They passed around money that Naccarato would later contribute to City Council races in a city where he didn't live.

But then the attorneys went to work on the charges, and in 2006 King County Superior Court Judge Michael Fox said prosecutors had misread the law: the state Public Disclosure Act did not allow for criminal charges. Frank, Al, and Stan were off the hook.

The money thing seemingly behind them, Frank and Frankie showed up one day in the summer of 2006 at Sugar's nudie club in Shoreline, full of themselves. They could go break the law all over the place now. They sat down in a room with the dancers crowded around them. Sex Economics 101 for strippers was under way. Object of the class: finesse more cash from consumers.

Sugar's was the least revenue producing of Frank's four clubs. It was smaller, older, and didn't quite have the hand-job reputation needed to draw a crowd. In 2006 it was bringing in just $37,000 a month, while Rick's in nearby Lake City was producing almost ten times that. The girls needed a lesson in Colacurcio capitalism.

As one of the club's dancers would later tell investigators, white-haired Frank, born in the midst of World War I, got up and, best as she could recall, told the gathering of young women: "If you give a hand job, charge for it. If you give a blow job, charge for it. If you don't charge for it, then you'll be fired." Then dapper Frankie, a child of the swingin' sixties, rose and repeated his father's time-tested mantra: Give free sex at your peril.

The cops and feds got a good chuckle when they heard of the Two Franks show. But they were still serious about following the money. As an investigator reported around that time, Conte was continuing his money runs to and from the apartment, the office, and the bank. "Conte exited the car carrying a handful of cash," the investigator said. "A few minutes later, he exited the bank and drove directly to Talents West." It was tedious, repetitious. And investigators watched almost every moment of it, their probe now having stretched from 2004 into 2007.

Something big was cooking. But Frank was distracted. By a six-to-three vote, the Washington Supreme Court reinstated the Strippergate charges. Justice Barbara Madsen said the law, which "helps to ensure the integrity of government by preventing disproportionate or controlling influence by financially strong groups," neither expressly allows nor explicitly bars criminal prosecution. So the case could continue.

The law had caught up with Frank yet again. So had a lesser-known part of his past.

Cold Cases, Partly Thawed

**"It just drew more police attention to the stripper business.
That's why he got killed."**

F rank's public persona was that of a tough but nonviolent "charmer"—one reporter used that word in a profile of him. But that wasn't always how he came off to the media, such as the day during Strippergate when he told a TV photographer, "I'll take that camera away from you pretty quick!" if the photographer didn't stop taking Frank's picture (he stopped). Then there was an incident that took place one night in the eighties outside the Firelite, his topless joint typically crowded beyond capacity.

In view of several reporters waiting to get in, a big man began drunkenly banging on the door, tired of waiting. Suddenly, the glass in the door shattered and flew into the club. The big guy stepped back, surprised at what he'd done. In a split second, Frank was out the door.

"You broke the window!" he said to the guy who was seemingly twice his size. "Hey . . ." the guy said, holding out his hands and apparently beginning to apologize. Frank raised a long metal rod in the air—he had walked out the door, bootlegging it behind him. Whack, whack! The big guy was on the pavement, screaming, holding his bloody hands over his battered face as Frank continued to raise the rod to full extension over him. He stroked it like a golf club on the customer's head and back.

"Stop! Don't hit me no more!" the guy pleaded, crying. He just went in his pants, he said.

Just then, two beat cops came through the crowd. Frank put the rod down against his backside again. The cops looked at Frank, then at the bloodied man cowering on the pavement.

"Hey, Frank," one said with a smile and a wave. "This guy giving you trouble?"

The bum broke my window, Frank said.

"We'll take care of it," one of the cops said. They got him up off the walk and led him down the street, bloodied and looking like someone happy to be arrested. (They sent him to the hospital.)

No one has been able to pin any killings on Frank, although federal and local investigators have been trying to do just that. In May 2007 the *Seattle Times* did take a bold stab at it with its own investigation. Under the headline "The Cops Vs. Colacurcio—the Last Round," reporters Steve Miletich and Jim Brunner wrote a mostly unsourced story about the "execution-style slayings of five people who had crossed [Frank]":

> The victims: a rival strip-club operator and his fiancée, a bar owner in Central Washington, a mechanic in a murder-for-hire scheme, and a police informant.
>
> The slayings, which took place in the 1970s and 1980s, have drawn little attention for more than twenty years.
>
> Now, federal and local investigators have reopened the cases, trying to find out once and for all whether Colacurcio had anything to do with the deaths. Most recently, investigators reopened the slain-informant case, which might offer them their best hope.

Authorities had already made arrests in four of the killings, the *Times* reported, but had not directly connected Frank or his associates to them. The slaying victims included Frank's Seattle topless club rival Frank "Sharkey" Hinkley, forty-five, and his girlfriend Barbara Rosenfeld, forty-four, found shot to death in 1975 inside Hinkley's Bear Cave bar in Seattle. Hinkley, who constantly ran afoul of the law—he was cited for lewd activity nearly two-hundred times—became the first Seattle strip club owner to convert to soda pop. "My flea-bag place is packed every night until two-thirty," he said after the conversion in the seventies. "Some guys come in and spend their whole pay-check." That helped him buy two Cadillacs and one Edmonds home with a swimming pool, twelve-foot bathtub, dance floor, sauna, and view of Puget Sound. He'd also earned the animosity of some of his rivals, investigators thought.

In a short interview, Frank waved off the probe as the usual malarkey. Cops had a habit of trying to pin their unsolved crimes on him, he said. "They have been investigating me since the time I was born."

What brought this on? Strippergate, Frank and Frankie's emboldened move to buy a City Hall favor. If Frank wanted to resurrect old tactics, then authorities would resurrect old cases and maybe end his lawbreaking ways.

But while they produced new testimony, clues, and the convictions of others, the revived investigations left Frank, as usual, untouched. That was the outcome of another cold-case probe as well.

The pajama-clad body of Seattle labor leader Mario Vaccarino was discovered seasoned with Parmesan cheese and floating face-down in his bathtub on October 24, 1985, at his Shorewood home in south King County. He had been violently drowned, his head held underwater, the medical examiner concluded. His year-old Buick was found parked at a McDonald's restaurant in White

Frank "Sharkey" Hinkley outside the Lucky Lady Tavern, January 1973.
Investigators tried unsuccessfully to link his death to Frank Colacurcio.
(Photo: Jerry Gay/ *The Seattle Times*)

Center, and his wallet was left in a tavern men's room. It was a
dramatically staged murder. Twenty-five years after his death,
he had joined the list of bar owners and others whose cold cases
investigators had been trying to link to Frank Colacurcio.

"We're reviewing all those cases," King County Sheriff's
detective Scott Tompkins confirmed in a 2009 interview. His
cold-case team worked with the Seattle and federal task forces
probing the murders detailed in the *Times* but was pursing the

union case separately. "Vaccarino's death is one we're actively trying to solve," he said, and Frank was among the usual suspects.

This is what's known: Vaccarino, sixty-one, head of Hotel Employees and Restaurant Employees (HERE) union Local 8, may have been killed by a man who ended up sentenced to prison for another murder. Or he was the man who at least hired the hit man. A Colacurcio associate who had heard underworld talk about the murder originally provided the somewhat sketchy details to *Seattle Weekly* and said he thought the killer was still in prison in Alaska.

But was Frank in any way involved? The Colacurcio associate didn't think so. And according to newspaper stories from the era, the trail had actually led away from Colacurcio, who was among many angry restaurant owners who had cause to dislike the not exactly lovable Vaccarino. "What we're learning," a police investigator said then, "is that there are fifty people with a motive for killing him." Fred Peitz, who took over as business agent for the union, pointed out, "There were some people who liked him and some people who hated him. That was true professionally and personally."

Vaccarino's former fiancée, Rhonda Hiller, who became a union international vice president, took control of Local 8 as a trustee, vowing to clean up the labor messes Vaccarino left behind, including a $200,000 debt and dwindling membership. She was saddened by his death but also remembered him as a sometimes-violent housemate. Court records show she and her twelve-year-old son from a previous marriage moved out of the home she shared with Vaccarino after he physically attacked her. "I thought my nose was broken, my lip was swollen, and I was in a lot of pain and my head hurt," she reported, recalling also how he would "push me, spit at me, slap me, and on at least one occasion, choke me."

The U.S. Senate Permanent Subcommittee on Investigations found that organized crime had infiltrated HERE's international union, and Vaccarino's name had come up in a federal probe of a New Jersey union linked to organized crime. Yet wouldn't a mob contract killer use a gun? Doesn't the grated cheese, car theft, and dumping of the wallet indicate some kind of amateur night antics? That's what the Colacurcio source thought. "He was supposed to just go to Mario's house and rough him up, but took it too far. He ended up putting the body in the tub and sprinkling it with Parmesan to suggest it was an Italian mob killing." The medical examiner concluded death was by drowning, and that indeed may have been the ultimate cause, the source said. But Vaccarino had fought back while getting roughed up, and it all ended in the bathroom. You don't just walk into a house and fill a tub, the source said, then say "step in so I can kill you." In the end, the source concluded—contrary to investigators' ongoing suspicions today—that Frank had no demonstrable hand in Vaccarino's death.

Frank would say only that those kinds of stories kept him entertained. His group's not a mob and he had nothing to do with any killings, period, he said. "I've given them [prosecutors] every chance to prove it," he said. "They're still trying, I guess."

Getting Frank

"It's an organization that has made its money on the backs of women. It's about violence and organized crime. It's not about the morals police."

With the murder claims going nowhere, the task force had quietly begun tapping Frank Colacurcio's phones and poking through his trash. They seized his bank records and set up surveillance outside his clubs. They were going through his life, looking for something, anything, to Get Frank. They had also stepped up their surveillance of Gil Conte, following his black Town Car around Lake City, including to his regular stops at the apartment on 24th Avenue Northwest. Originally a six-unit apartment building, a seventh unit was later added to the structure, accessible from an outside door. Apartment A was registered to Conte.

Between May 29 and August 6, 2007, the ex–lounge singer was recorded going into Apartment A on forty-two separate occasions. The feds laboriously wrote down the details of each visit. "He arrived and departed in the Town Car on each occasion," one investigator reported. "During ten of those visits, Conte carried an object either in or out of the apartment building": a bag, an envelope, a paper sack. The feds wondered if he was hiding Frank's money there. This went on, month after month, each coming and going observed by probers, viewing Conte as he opened and closed his door, opened and closed his truck, went in and exited the apartment, and drove away. Conte went in and out fifteen times in the first few weeks of January 2008. The apartment trips had been going on for four years and now seemed to be increasing, becoming a great interest to probers.

That same month, Frank put Strippergate behind him, more or less. Both Frank and son Frankie copped to felony and misdemeanor charges in the campaign finance scandal, admitting to providing funds to reimburse donors. Once facing more than a decade in prison under the original charges, each was allowed to plead out and pay $10,000 fines, then walk away apparent winners. They each also paid $55,000 to settle a separate city Ethics and Elections Commission complaint that they hid campaign donations. Conte, the money deliveryman, pleaded guilty to a misdemeanor charge of conspiring with the Colacurcios and was fined $1,000. County Prosecuting Attorney Dan Satterberg, who took over after Norm Maleng died in 2007, said, "Sometimes you have to know when to declare victory and to move on."

To some, it was never much of a scandal—certainly not on par with the endless and entrenched corruption of Chicago or New York. For most of five years, the Franks had lied about the campaign bundling. Frankie, for example, said it was all about political activism. "For ages," he told the *P-I*'s Lewis Kamb with a straight face, "I've been encouraging people to get involved in politics, because I think it's one of the fundamental rights in America. That's my only crime." Frankie said he encouraged everyone he knew to donate to the three City Council members because they had "impressed" him at fund-raisers. Likewise, Frank said his son was getting a bad rap because of the family name. "It looks bad for him because I was a bad guy and now they're trying to make him a bad guy," he said. "In the paper, all these years they printed me as a bad guy. But he's like a cream puff, you know what I mean?"

Yet as a result of the plea bargain, Frankie had to finally confess the truth. In his King County Superior Court admission, he wrote:

> Between November 11, 2002, and September 12, 2003, my father, myself, and others agreed to provide reimbursements to various individuals we knew were willing to make campaign contributions to support various candidates seeking election to the Seattle City Council. In March, 2003, and as a part of this agreement, I provided money to my then wife she then gave to my then-sister in law and her employer to reimburse them for $600.00 campaign contributions they each made to Ms. Heidi Wills, a candidate for the Seattle City Council. I understood that candidates for the Seattle City Council, including Ms. Wills, were required to report the identity of person making campaign contributions. By causing the two people identified above to be reimbursed for the campaign contributions they made, I caused the Wills' campaign to file a report that falsely identified my former sister-in-law and her employer as contributors to her campaign when in fact I provided the money for those contributions. All of my acts in this regard occurred in King County, Washington. I admit to the foregoing facts and plead guilty to Counts I, IV and V of the information which the State filed against me in July, 2005.

And though Frankie got much of the blame in the press for Strippergate, Frank's little-noticed confession, filed days later, detailed a much more central role by the old man:

Between November 11, 2002 and September 12, 2003 I agreed with others, including my son, to give money to people we knew who were willing to contribute to Seattle City Council candidates' campaigns. In May 2003, I gave money to attorney Walt Dauber, and requested that he and his law partners make a contribution to Judy Nicastro, a candidate for the Seattle City Council. I also gave money to Stan Naccarato for the same purpose. Although I was not aware at the time of City Council candidates' reporting requirements, I understand that Ms. Nicastro was required to report the identity of contributors and that in reimbursing others, I caused the Nicastro campaign to file a report that falsely identified others as contributors to her campaign when in fact I provided the money for those contributions.

In the confession and sentencing documents, Harley Anders, an investigator for the Seattle Ethics and Elections Commission and a former FBI agent, provided more details:

Witnesses say that Frank Colacurcio Jr. uses credit cards for some purchases, but pays cash for most things that he purchases, including furniture and cars. During her marriage to Frank Colacurcio Jr., Teena Colacurcio Hines received $2,000 per week cash spending money from her husband. . . . In March 2003 Teena Colacurcio Hines collected two $600 checks for the campaign of Heidi Wills from her sister Jennifer Opheim-Palmateer and her sister's employer, Jeff Carney at the motorcycle business owned by Mr. Carney. Hines reimbursed them with cash in exchange for the checks. The cash Hines gave them had been given to her by Frank Colacurcio Jr. Hines delivered the two checks to Frank Colacurcio Jr. . . .

As for father Frank, said Anders, he had given Walt Dauber $1,300 and his law partners $1,950 to pass along to the Judy Nicastro campaign. He gave Stan Naccarato, known in Tacoma as "Mr. Baseball" for his support of local teams, another $1,300 to do the same.

> This occurred at the Emerald Queen Casino at a "fight night" when Mr. Naccarato was socializing with his long time friends Frank Colacurcio Sr., Albert Rosellini and [Colacurcio club operator] Steve Fueston. Albert Rosellini states that he did not reimburse anyone in cash for contributions to any of the 2003 Seattle City Council campaigns. He also states that he did not see anyone give cash to Mr. Naccarato at the fight night. Steve Fueston states that he did not reimburse Mr. Naccarato . . . [but] says that Frank Colacurcio Sr. often carries significant amounts of cash and that on many occasions Mr. Fueston has seen Frank Colacurcio Sr. give Mr. Naccarato large sums of cash or pay large sums of cash for dinner and drinks . . .

Naccarato, it seems, wasn't sure who gave what to whom. Maybe he was reimbursed for up to $700, he thought. But, as he told Anders, at age seventy-seven, he had health problems that "impair his memory." However, he had earlier told the *News Tribune* of Tacoma that he made the contribution at the urging of his "good friend" Al Rosellini.

The plea deal stretched Frank's record to seven felonies over seven decades: statutory rape, felony assault, bingo racketeering, three tax raps (one reversed), and Strippergate. But at least he could throw up his hands and say, at last, *done!* with this bullshit scandal. He could rededicate his life to sex. "He gets laid every night by one of the dancers," said one of his office workers and job interviewers, Bobby Payton, who also stayed at Frank's house. Of course, "he has the money" for it, Payton said.

Frankie, meanwhile, could get back to taking over. After a quarter century of study, the son was assuming more of the father's political, as well as managerial, role. Criminally influencing

Seattle City Council matters had been a step up for Frankie after years of sparring with suburban cities over club locations and operations. He took several of them to court over the four-foot rule—imposed to separate dancer from customer—and pulled a Frank-like stunt when he bid $3,000 at a charity auction to have lunch with Shoreline police chief Denise Pentony. She called it "inappropriate" and ate alone.

Unfortunately, Frankie's big Seattle adventure came with a hidden cost. In his father's heyday, payoffs and kickbacks were a secret but acceptable way to get things done. A rezone back then wouldn't have required much more than a lunch bag of cash left on the bar. Yet Frankie's bold assault on a supposedly cleaned-up election system made people mad. That was most evident five months later, at a stunning June 2008 press conference. For most of three years, the local/federal task force had been compiling the criminal biography of Frank and his people. And now they were about to tell the story—while also moving to seize Frank's properties. They were also preparing to indict him and the others if it came to that, said Seattle police chief Gil Kerlikowske.

The chief's features hardened like poured concrete as he spoke of Strippergate and Frank's sexual profiteering, including charging his dancers to dance. "Let me be really clear about this part. . . . It's an organization that has made its money on the backs of women. It's about violence and organized crime," said the chief, who has since been appointed by President Obama as U.S. drug czar. "It's not about the morals police." City, county, state, and federal officials had mounted "the most significant organized-crime investigation we have ever undertaken," Kerlikowske said. "It has been a great investigation into an organization that has done considerable damage to this city [and] to its electoral process."

U.S. Attorney Jeffrey Sullivan said investigators had spoken with several hundred witnesses and logged endless hours of recorded phone calls, surveillance video, and listening-device intercepts from Frank's operations. Much of the dirty details were laid out in a search warrant signed by Corey Cote. An FBI agent for fourteen years, Cote had been on Frank's trail for much of the decade. After four years with the agency's international terrorism squad, he seemed qualified to go after Frank, the local warlord.

"Although he is not officially listed as an owner of Talents West or any of the four strip clubs," said Cote, "Colacurcio Sr. provides guidance and oversight to the other subjects with respect to all aspects of managing the business. On important issues, Colacurcio Sr. appears to have ultimate decision-making authority over the operation of the clubs and Talents West."

It was a criminal enterprise, he said. Perhaps they had finally broken the hermetic seal around it.

Nudity Inc., Inside Out

As one of the club co-owners told a lowly paid dancer who
wasn't gung ho about sex with strangers, "Well honey,
you've got to get in there and compete."

In a voluminous search warrant, FBI agent Corey Cote detailed
how Frank's organization operated and how it made as much as
$12 million a year doing it. Son Frankie, as a co-owner, handled
the daily paperwork and cash flow, reconciling discrepancies in
revenue and receipts. Frank's nephew Leroy Christiansen did
some of the same duties and was also a co-owner, along with
longtime partners Dave Ebert and Steve Fueston. Gil Conte,
Frank's former driver and friend, was the trusted money man,
picking up the day's receipts at the clubs and driving them to
the Talents West offices. Julie McDowell had been a dancer and
then manager at Rick's for more than two decades, in charge
of the girls, while bookkeeper Marsha Furfaro kept track of
the debts run up by dancers. Talents West had run Sugar's in
Shoreline since 1982 and the other clubs—Honey's in Everett,
Fox's in Parkland, and Rick's, the largest and most profitable, in
Seattle—since 1988.

At each of the four clubs, Cote said, "prostitution is rampant." Dancers regularly were paid to engage in sex with customers, knowingly permitted by club managers. Frank and the owners received a cut from the illegal sex and benefited from the other revenue—the cover charge and soft drinks—generated by customers lured in by the sex. Taken together, this working relationship amounted to criminal conspiracy and racketeering, Cote said, based on evidence gathered by cops and agents posing as customers and employees. One female undercover agent was hired as a waitress and soon worked into a management position, all in a two-month stint. Five dancers who had already been paid as confidential informants by the cops were further employed to provide dirt for the task force. Several agreed reluctantly, it seems, agreeing to cooperate in return for dropping prostitution, drug, and morals charges. A man with inside knowledge of the business operations also provided details after receiving $500 for providing "historical information" about Frank's operation. Several other dancers initiated contacts with police to tell what they knew, said Cote.

Rick's was officially owned by Christiansen, Ebert, Fueston, and Frankie, according to testimony Fueston gave in another court case. For 365 days a year, customers flooded through the doors, doling out a $10 cover and observing the mandatory one-drink minimum, another five bills. The nearly eighty dancers who revolved through Rick's and across its two stages usually paid $130 daily rent for the privilege to dance. At a less-popular club such as Sugar's, the rent was around $75. Their income was made off customers who paid for private dances, particularly those in the darkly lighted VIP area with mostly hidden booths. Undercover cops watched customers have sex with girls and then leave condoms on the floor. Customers used their credit cards to buy tokens—Frank's funny money—which were used like poker chips to pay for dances and drinks, tips and sex. The tokens were interchangeable at all four clubs. When performers cashed in the tokens, Frank and Co. took another 10 percent off the top. For example, said Cote, describing a typical transaction, "If a customer pays a dancer $50 for oral sex, the dancer will exchange the tokens for $45 and the club retains a $5 exchange fee."

The feds considered the token exchange to be money laundering. They also claimed Frank's club evaded city admission taxes by underreporting receipts from the cover charge. Rick's would keep its count through a camera mounted inside the door, making it possible to tally the daily number of entering customers. The video count was necessary, said Frank's bookkeeper Betty Howard in another court case, to make customer and money counts match up, so the admission tax could be correctly determined. "There have been employee theft problems in the past," she said, "and we avoid that now by reconciling receipts with attendance."

Investigators had their doubts and mounted their own video camera to a utility pole outside Rick's, said agent Cote. It was a gotcha moment. Over a ten-month period, Rick's reported about sixty thousand customers entering its doors. The feds' camera showed the count closer to 122,000. They figured the club had scammed the city for about $32,000 in unpaid admission taxes. Considering the clubs were million-dollar-monthly operations, that seemed a paltry amount when compared against the risk. But no revenue source went untouched, legit or otherwise. During just 2006, according to agent Cote, dancer rent produced $3.8 million revenue at Rick's alone. Hard-nosed managers still docked dancers their $130 even if they missed their shifts, the feds said. If dancers did show, but had a bad night financially, they were given a notice for the balance due.

Those who owed back rent, said Cote, were often the ones who didn't engage in sex. The clubs then used that as leverage, telling girls they had a better chance of paying what they owed if they'd just use their hands a little more. As one club manager told a lowly paid dancer who wasn't gung ho about sex with strangers, "Well honey, you've got to get in there and compete."

It had become clear to the task force that Frank was dominating the hand and breast market. He and his partners were raking in millions, Cote determined, after tracking credit card and ATM transactions at Rick's for a sixteen-month period. From January 2006 through April 2007, Rick's electronic cash flow came to $4.2 million. At Honey's, the transactions came to $2.3 million; Fox's was $2.1 million and Sugar's $600,000. For the four clubs, that's $9.2 million. Then there was the revenue from rent, chip exchanges, drinks, cover, and condoms—roughly another $6 million from the clubs. Led by Rick's $7 million total revenue during those months, Frank's four-club operation took in $15.2 million—close to $1 million a month, or $250,000 a week.

None of that money went to Frank—on the record, anyway. Cote and federal agents tracked $1.1 million in payments to Christiansen, Ebert, and Fueston each, with $1 million going to Frankie. But that was just the profits from Rick's. Christiansen, Ebert, and Fueston each got roughly another $850,000 from the other clubs' operations; Frankie got another $800,000. In sixteen months, each owner had made something close to $2 million.

To make this all work, said Cote, "the business model at each of the four strip clubs is the same." Nudity alone wouldn't bring in this kind of money, making sex the necessary component. "The essential element of this business model is the promotion and facilitation of prostitution," he said. Sex brings in more customers, thus more girls are needed to service them. That drives up the rent and the chip revenue. If the girls were there to be seen but not touched, said Cote, the clubs would be the poorer for it. Said one dancer at Sugar's, "If it wasn't for the sex, most of the guys wouldn't even come in."

The VIP areas at each club facilitated the money flow through masturbation, oral sex, fingering, and now and then intercourse, investigators discovered. Dances might generally cost $20 to $30; with sex, they would cost $50 or more—that included a "hand finish" as the girls called polishing the knob. "It doesn't make any difference if you come or not," said one dancer. "If I rub your dick, it will cost $50." Maybe less than half the girls at one club will engage in sex, and those who do, some engaging as many as a dozen men a night, don't necessarily do it all. "I'll rub you, I'll suck you," a dancer told a Pierce County undercover cop at Fox's. "But I won't fuck you."

Records confiscated by the feds indicate club managers moved some girls—most in their twenties, but one a forty-six-year-old mom—from club to club after they were busted. It was done to provide Frank and his partners with "plausible deniability" in cases such as the pending federal charges, said Cote. Frankie and his cousin Christiansen doled out little in the way of daily discipline, Cote claimed, and tended not to fire any employees for gross violations. Some records revealed thousands of dollars in loans and back rent owed by dancers. They were paying off their obligations at $10 or $20 a month, leaving them in constant debt to the clubs. Personnel records for girls who went by the stage names of Jada, Janika, and Gypsy (another changed her nom de guerre from Kerri to Carmela to Meadow and back to Kerri) show such hand-written entries as "blow job" and "hand job," and indicate the offender was moved to another club as a result. One dancer named Karma

Frank Colacurcio Sr., 90, pleads guilty at the King County Courthouse in Seattle in the Strippergate case, January 28, 2008. (Photo: Ellen M. Banner/ *The Seattle Times*)

was reprimanded for "Having sex with customer—no protection at all. Standard for her. Both parents died from AIDS." A manager wasted no words describing another dancer seen giving oral sex: "Regarding Tessa: Caught with cock in mouth." Frankie apparently appreciated the brevity. "We're all guys here," he said later, discussing the note with an undercover officer posing as a manager, "so you can just be brief and to the point."

For almost a year, Frank and the feds negotiated a plea or settlement to probable racketeering charges. It looked like an official indictment and trial would be avoidable if Frank and his partners gave up their dance joints—closed them, sold them, handed them over to the government for disposal—and disappeared.

"Frank's finally feeling his age," said an attorney familiar with the talks. "He's tired and weak." He was spending a good part of the day at home in his favorite leather chair, looking out at the lake as his ex-wife took care of the daily chores.

Nonetheless, he was strong enough to walk away from a settlement to head off an indictment in early 2009, keeping alive his, and a city's, extraordinary history of vice. "There's just nobody like this guy," the attorney said, shaking his head. "He's the last one."

Epilogue

In the summer of 2009, the feds formally announced the federal grand jury indictment of Frank, Frankie, Christiansen, Ebert, Fueston, and Conte, with a trial set for 2011. They were charged with fifteen counts of racketeering, conspiracy, mail fraud, and money laundering, facilitated by prostitution at their clubs, and faced up to twenty years in prison. All pleaded not guilty and vowed to fight on.

Obviously, having arrested an estimated 120 dancers for 150 lewd dance and prostitution violations over two years, local police and federal agents had spent considerable time and money to get Frank. Just the *index* of the evidence ran twenty-five pages. Among the material: a searchable CD containing more than 89,300 pages of documents; eight CDs with 15,989 pages of Rick's dancer records; a CD containing a 2,461-page database of telephone records and pen register (number-tracing) data; twenty-one CDs and DVDs containing audio files, video files, and digital photographs; and three CDs plus a 1.5 terabyte SATA computer hard drive containing electronic evidence downloaded from seized Talents West computers. There were also 275 boxes of documents stored at the Seattle FBI offices, along with discarded trash that agents had fished out of garbage cans and dumpsters, tax records, and 2,200 DVDs containing video "pole camera" footage that kept track of the number of customers entering and leaving the clubs. As well, there were approximately forty DVDs containing covert video and audio recordings made by dancers working as confidential informants inside the clubs.

Prosecutors said that, in addition to long prison terms, they were seeking a judgment as high as $25 million by seizure of the club properties, including the Talents West office and related real estate. "Our trial team has interviewed more than two hundred witnesses, reviewed thousands of pages of reports, transcripts of wire taps, and video surveillance of activities at the clubs," said U.S. Attorney Jeffrey Sullivan, a Bush appointee who was replaced in 2010 by Obama appointee Jenny Durkan. "We look forward to proving the RICO conspiracy in court." Frank's clubs constituted the largest prostitution organization in the state, Sullivan said. "A lot of malarkey" was Frank's unusually mild retort. He and the others all pleaded not guilty, although Frank had to struggle to get to court. His ailments included hypertension, gout, arthritis, bursitis, and a weakened heart—it was fifty years now since he'd had that first heart attack. His ex-wife, Jackie, seventy, who had divorced him sixteen years earlier while he was in prison, agreed to return to the Sheridan Beach home they once shared and provide care for him, taking over his bill paying and check writing as well.

The indictment against Frank and the others repeated much of the information made public a year earlier. But prosecutors did reveal more of the inner dialogue from Frank's clubs and offices. Clearly, a good time was being had by all. Or by Frankie, anyway. In March 2008 two dancers met with Frankie to complain about the relentless sex going on at Rick's. In particular, they bitched about a dancer who told a customer, "I'll give you every part of my body and you can stick your fingers all inside me." Frankie, they said, responded: "My type of girl." In another conversation, Frankie, as a matter of form, told a dancer that sex acts weren't officially condoned in the clubs. However, he said, it was OK to have sex in his office.

Late in 2009 Conte surprised a lot of people by stepping out from Frank's crowd and pleading guilty to one count of conspiracy to use interstate facilities in aid of racketeering. It looked like he'd been turned and took a plea under an agreement to rat out Frank. Conte has been so close to his mentor that he even once appeared in a picture in the *Seattle Times* posing as Frank—after fooling a photographer. In 2010 Conte, seventy-six, was handed a year's probation and had to give up financial interest in Sugar's, which was shut down as part of the deal. He also was barred from going into any other Colacurcio clubs in the future. It was a soft landing because, prosecutors said, Frank and the others made millions off the strip biz, but Conte not so much: he was effectively broke and living on unemployment. "Mr. Conte was situated differently than the other individual defendants charged in this matter," prosecutors said in court papers. "Specifically, Mr. Conte was paid only a modest salary for his work at the Talents West strip clubs, and thus he did not profit from the criminal enterprise to the same extent as the other defendants. Moreover, as compared to the other defendants, Mr. Conte had less decision-making authority within the businesses." Conte had a modest musician's union pension and Social Security to help out, but told the court he was too broke to pay a fine—and none was assessed. Conte's attorney Richard Hansen said his client played a minor role for Colacurcio, and in a letter to the court, Conte's son Vincent called his dad "a big-hearted honest person, and I believe that is why Frank trusted him to collect the money, knowing he wouldn't steal." Though Conte was also not to have contact with any of the club owners or employees, he was granted specific permission to continue to have "non-case-related contact" with his old friend Frank and son Frankie. There was no indication he would have to testify against his friends at the scheduled 2011 racketeering trial.

Frankie, meanwhile, had married again, to a woman named Rainee, only to end up back in court facing off with one of his former wives, Teena. Though prosecutors had said he was making $100,000 a month a few years earlier, Frankie claimed he was close to broke, had lost his strip club job and income, and thus couldn't pay child support for his and Teena's three kids. He and his father had agreed to a pretrial release condition that prevented them from entering their clubs or working in the strip business, so he was looking for work, he said, but couldn't find employment even as a gas station attendant. "I do not have a college education and my only employment has been in the adult entertainment business," he explained. Talents West had also closed down Sugar's in Shoreline and moved employees to the three other clubs.

Teena wasn't buying Frankie's sob story. He owned two houses, she said, and four cars. His income has "always been" between $1 million and $2 million, she said. "It is far from the truth that Frank is now penniless," added Teena, who was unable to pay her $738 water bill and had received a shutoff notice. Frankie "is only doing this as a front for his case . . . to show federal prosecutors that he has no money." Frankie had stopped paying his $9,000 monthly child support immediately after his indictment, claiming, "My business associates have essentially locked me out of all my businesses and cut off all of my income." Even new wife Rainee was working part-time to make ends meet, he said. Mother Jackie jumped into the dispute as well. She was paying the children's costs to attend private school, she said, and buying groceries for her poor son and daughter-in-law. "For example, Costco recently had a sale on chickens. I bought more than I needed so that I could pass those on to my son." She was also making payments on two of his cars, she said. Teena thought her ex could pay the back child support by at least selling one of his freakin' cars. (Frankie has always collected cars, along with a lengthy list of traffic fines for speeding.) Apparently he did sell a $40,000 car—which he let go to his mother-in-law for $2,000, Teena said. But she didn't see any of that money and thought it was a sham anyway. As of this writing, the dispute continues.

So did the action at Rick's, at least for awhile. Prosecutors said an undercover sting operation done months after the indictment determined that acts of prostitution were still routinely taking place at Rick's as well as the Everett club, Honey's. During eight postindictment visits to the clubs, cops and FBI agents reported being propositioned by ten dancers. One performer said a new hands-off policy had briefly gone into effect, "but it didn't last very long and things are [now] better than ever." Ebert and Fueston, unlike Frankie and Frank, had been allowed to continue overseeing Talents West operations. But prosecutors asked that control be put in government hands because the vice violations were ongoing. Ebert claimed he had in fact fired ten dancers for sex violations, and Fueston said the feds had seemingly become obsessed with nailing Frank and his partners for something they really couldn't control. "Historically," said his attorney in a court brief, "prostitution has occurred in and around adult entertainment establishments, regardless of location or ownership. Mr. Fueston and the codefendants are no more responsible for this fact of life than they are for inventing the world's 'oldest profession.'" So gung ho was the government,

Fueston's attorney said, that it had "transformed the Federal Bureau of Investigation, an agency capable of investigating matters of national significance such as capital federal offenses, espionage, and international terrorism, into a vice squad."

But it all turned out to be legal posturing. In April 2010 Christiansen, sixty-seven, Ebert, sixty-two, and Fueston, sixty-two, who held title to Frank's nudie properties, all pleaded guilty to racketeering and prostitution charges and agreed to turn over the four clubs, valued at $4.5 million, to the feds in return for probationary sentences. "We are shutting down a corrupt criminal organization that made millions of dollars exploiting women," said new U.S. Attorney Jenny Durkan. "These clubs cast shadows far beyond the neighborhoods where they were located." In the early morning hours of May 6, the doors to Rick's, Honey's, and Fox's were closed and locked. Sugar's had already been shut down as part of the Conte plea.

In June Frankie, forty-eight, took a deal as well. In return for his guilty plea and the dropping of all but the racketeering conspiracy charge, prosecutors agreed to recommend a 366-day prison term and three years of supervised release, during which time Frankie would be barred from employment or management in the adult entertainment industry. He also agreed to forfeit to the U.S. government all rights to club properties including the Talents West building and to hand over $1.3 million in cash. Frankie's attorney, John Wolfe, contended his client "had no greater involvement" than his partners but couldn't get a similar walk-away deal because he was Frank's son. Prosecutor Durkan saw no reason for leniency, describing the Colacurcio's lustful crime history as a "fifty-year scourge on the community."

The plea agreements had been ongoing for a year and were no surprise to insiders. But it was a stunning, historic conclusion nonetheless: for the first time since Frank introduced topless dancing to Seattle in the early sixties, the Stripper King's last clubs had gone out of business.

But had Frank?

Authorities had been after him almost since the invention of penicillin. He vowed never to retire "until I'm in the grave." And on June 18, 2010—his ninety-third birthday—he defiantly challenged the federal case against him. He asked a judge to dismiss the charges, arguing they conflicted with state law and could be unconstitutional. His attorney also filed a sealed document on Frank's health status indicating Colacurcio was gravely ill.

Everyone else, including his son, could take a plea. Not old Frank. No way were the feds going to win the final round. He would fight to the last death rattle, if necessary.

Exactly two weeks later, on the morning of July 2, 2010, Frank won.

He retired.

Death was due to heart failure. All charges against him were subsequently dismissed. The massive case and a singular ribald life were suddenly over.

"It is the end of an era," said former U.S. attorney Jeffrey Sullivan, "hopefully one that won't be repeated."

But rival clubs were already expanding and several new strip clubs had sprung up around Seattle. Other would-be Franks jockeyed to make a bid on his shuttered clubs forfeited to the government.

One-of-a-kinds don't repeat. But they do live on.

Bibliography

Breslin, Jimmy. *The Gang That Couldn't Shoot Straight*. New York: Viking Adult, 1969.

Chambliss, William J. *On the Take: From Petty Crooks to Presidents*, 2nd ed. Bloomington: Indiana University Press, 1988.

Corr, O. Casey. *KING: The Bullitts of Seattle and Their Communications Empire*. Seattle: University of Washington Press, 1996.

de Barros, Paul. *Jackson Street After Hours*. Seattle: Sasquatch Books, 1993.

Donnelly, Robert C. "Organizing Portland." *Oregon Historical Quarterly*, Fall 2003.

Eaves, Elisabeth. *Bare: The Naked Truth About Stripping*. Berkeley, CA: Seal Press, 2004.

Hughes, John C. and Ryan Teague Beckwith. *On the Harbor: From Black Friday to Nirvana*. Las Vegas: Stephens Press, 2005.

Kelly, Pat and Jerry Sampont. "Relics from the Past." Seattle Police Guild *Guardian*, October 2007.

LaRosa, Paul. *Tacoma Confidential: A True Story of Murder, Suicide, and a Police Chief's Secret Life*. New York: Signet, 2006.

Lee, Gypsy Rose and Erik Preminger. *Gypsy: Memoirs of America's Most Celebrated Stripper*. Berkeley, CA: Frog Books, 1999.

Matthews, Todd. "Wah Mee" (year-long serialized feature). *Asian Focus*, 1999.

Morgan, Murray. *Skid Road: An Informal Portrait of Seattle*. Seattle: University of Washington Press, 1981.

Pepper, William F. *An Act of State: The Execution of Martin Luther King*. New York: Verso, 2003.

Pileggi, Nicholas. *Wiseguy: Life in a Mafia Family*. New York: Pocket Books, 1985.

Smith, Payton. *Rosellini: Immigrants' Son and Progressive Governor*. Seattle: University of Washington Press, 1997.

Stanford, Phil. *Portland Confidential: Sex, Crime, and Corruption in the Rose City*. Portland, OR: Westwinds Press, 2004.

Index

Index

Acknowledgments

With appreciation for the source work and/or assistance of those not otherwise called out in the earlier pages: Ross Anderson, Ken Armstrong, James Aston, Skip Berger, Jack Broom, Mike Carter, Dick Clever, Gary Cluff, Lou Corsaletti, Dan Crawford, Walt Crowley, Mary Beth Edenholm, Tim Egan, Mark Fefer, Paul Henderson, Janet Horne, Tony Johnson, Steve Johnston, Red Kelly, Gary Kennedy, Erik Lacitis, Dick Larsen, Casey McNerthney, Kim Murphy, Eric Nalder, Dee (Hacksaw) Norton, Jack Olsen, Levi Pulkkinen, Joey Solman, Ken Schram, Mike Seely, Chuck Taylor, Bob Young. A special thanks to those who can't be named.

Portions of this material appeared in another form in *Seattle Weekly*.

About the Author

Rick Anderson is a staff writer at *Seattle Weekly* and former news columnist for the *Seattle Post-Intelligencer* and the *Seattle Times*, where he won the Haywood Broun Award for columns about the underdog. He is the winner of the 2010 Association of Alternative Newsweeklies national award for news reporting, and is included in *The Best American Crime Reporting 2010*. He is also the author of *Home Front: The Government's War on Soldiers*. His work has appeared in *Mother Jones*, the *Village Voice*, and Salon.com. He lives in Seattle.